Gloria

Ramblings

of a

Curious Man

all of your work in
getting this in shape to
publish.

Clare
Nov 6/2015

aka Mac.

Clare McCarthy

Published by
Mac Press,
30 Elm Ave., Orangeville,
ON Canada L9W 3G4

Front cover illustration by Glen Godfrey

ISBN 978-0-9877826-1-8

10 9 8 7 6 5 4 3 2 1

Ramblings
of a
Curious Man

Clare McCarthy

Clare in 1945 in Gold Centre

TABLE OF CONTENTS

Ramblings of a Peripatetic Man....................1

1 Too Stubborn To Die 3

2 Mind Over Matter 10

3 An Illustrious Gene Pool 16

4 Willie's World....................................24

5 Kid Stuff...34

6 Remembering Radio 38

7 A Maverick Both Profane And Profound44

8 On the Move Again 53

9 Dunnville High School Daze....................60

10 The Perfesser at Work........................65

11 Doctor, Lawyer, Indian Chief, ...70

Supreme Court Judge............................70

12 Tote that Barge, Lift that Bale................75

13 When the Rubber Hit the Road 81

14 Intoxicating Prose............................91

15 The School of Hard Knocks...................97

16 Off to the Amazon Jungle...................111

17 Land of Ice and Fire.........................128

18 Into the Land of Big Feet...................130

19 The Lure of the North 138

20 A Chip Off The Old Block 142

21 Two Thousand Pounds 146

of Bacon and Bone..............................146

22 A River Runs Through It 150

23 More Philosophical Ponderings............156

24 Leaner and Meaner 164

25 Crazy as an Outhouse Rat....................167

26 Sausages & Eggs Over Easy...................169

and the French Connection....................169

27 The Best Laid Plans 172

28 The Times They Are A-Changin'............177

29 Gone But Not Forgotten....................180

30 The McCarthy Diaspora 191

31 So What? 194

Mac, A Minnie Biography 199

Acknowledgements 202

Ramblings of a Peripatetic Man

When a friend referred to me as peripatetic, I wasn't sure whether it was an insult or complement, nor did I even know how the Hell to spell the word. The Concise Oxford Dictionary provides the following definition: "Walking from place to place, so called from Aristotle's custom of walking in Lyceum while teaching." This habit of Aristotle suggests a person who is always on the move and describes my occupation as a High School teacher for thirty-four years wandering in front of a class while I taught.

1 Too Stubborn To Die

At the age of forty, near the beginning of a new school year, Saturday September 8, 1979 was the day that allowed me to experience the feeling of being a spectator at my own funeral. It was just after six in the evening as I pedaled leisurely westward up an incline on highway #9 just outside of Orangeville. A blinding setting sun and distractions by her two children caused a young woman's car to slam into the rear of my bicycle. The impact, which folded my rear wheel up to the seat post, shot me through the air like a human cannonball in a circus.

The collision fractured several ribs which punctured both of my lungs causing them to collapse like a two-dollar suitcase in the rain. My damaged carcass skidded through the gravel along the edge of the road and bounced to a stop.

When a police officer arrived at the accident scene, he reported that my bicycle was welded to the front of the lady's automobile. Such a novel hood ornament did not come without cost to my fractured anatomy! Fortunately a good- Samaritan in the guise of a nurse who lived nearby appeared and administered first-aid until an ambulance showed up. The medics transported me to the Orangeville Hospital Emergency ward, and doctors stabilized my condition before sending me aloft in helicopter air ambulance, 'Bandage One' headed for the trauma unit of Toronto's Sunnybrook Hospital.

My wife knew I had gone cycling after supper but she attributed my tardy return to the likelihood that I had stopped to visit a friend, and had lost track of time whilst gabbing. Ironically as 'Bandage One' flew over Orangeville, my wife Dorothy stood outside with a neighbour as the two speculated on the plight of what poor soul was sending the aircraft on   another emergency mission. It was not until she went up to our bedroom and saw my wallet lying on the bed that she realized I'd gone out without any identification. Dorothy then remembered I usually carried a bit of cash in the pocket of my track suit to buy a drink or snack. Since I had not been wearing a helmet at the time of my accident, my most serious injury as diagnosed by Sunnybrook chief neurosurgeon Dr. Charles Tater was a subdural haematoma or bruise on the brain in layman's language. The car's impact had bounced my brain off the inside of my skull causing the bruising and subdural hemorrhaging which generated increased intracranial pressure. To relieve the stress, it was necessary to drill burr holes in my skull while doctors at Sunnybrook in charge of the healing process kept me in a temporary induced coma by the administration of the tropical drug curare.

Much later, my twisted cartoonist mind pictured me propped up in a hospital bed with a target painted on my arse and the curare being administered by a pint size medical man imported from the Amazon jungle. No doubt he used a blowgun to fire curare tipped darts into my backside rather than follow the common North American practice of administering the drug via a hypodermic needle.

As I lounged in a Sunnybrook Hospital bed, it was not until the morning following the accident that my wife, through local police was able to track me down. When Dorothy, and sweating friend Gus, entered my hospital room, they had no idea what to expect. Since I was connected to a ventilator which did my breathing, the collection of wires and tubes necessary to keep my functions functioning must have looked like a plumber's nightmare. Being in a comatose state, I did not respond when my wife gripped my hand. It took several weeks as a patient before I was able to wiggle even a finger, thus acknowledging my ability to react. Several injuries were left untreated, being considered minor, as the chief concern was to control my cranial contusions, and keep me alive.

My only thought while recovering was, "I must survive. There were too many things that I had not done yet." I guess I was just too stubborn to die! The rumour mill at home, knowing I was in a coma, generated nonsense to the effect that if I did survive, I would be as a vegetable. Even though I didn't cash in my chips as a result of the accident, when I returned home and could have visitors, seeing the response of others, I felt as though I was actually a spectator at my own funeral. Some friends responded as I anticipated and several others did not but I was pleasantly surprised by the concern of those who I thought might not be that interested in my recovery.

The recovery process was a slow, prolonged and incremental one (and is probably still continuing). Following the accident, I spent my time in bed simply resting. Until my lungs were back in working order, a respirator did my breathing via a tube through my throat. Unable to speak, I attempted to communicate by writing in a hard covered notebook. Since my writing at that time was more a scrawl than legible script, I was often frustrated when those to whom I was trying to communicate were unable to interpret my hieroglyphics. Over time my scribbling became slightly more legible but relief from the breathing tube in my throat was definitely a step forward in my recovery process allowing me to speak normally.

I was eventually taken at times in a wheelchair to the bathroom, and was allowed to sit in a bedside chair. I do recall using a chest-high walker without wheels to prop myself up vertically. I could then shuffle without actually being able to walk but was at least able to stand.

Those in charge of treating my head injuries and breathing, left a right shoulder separation as it was, treating it as a relatively minor problem. My left big toe however did require some repair work. Since my feet at the time of the accident were strapped in place by rat-trap pedals, when the collision catapulted me off my bicycle, this caused my left big toe to end up pointing upward, bent at the last joint. The suggested correction was to repair my damaged appendage by severing the tendon, thus straightening out the toe, then fusing the joint. All of the drilling and mechanics of fusing the toe was completed under the influence of a local anesthetic. I could thus enjoy the sound of the surgeon grinding the bone and drilling a hole to insert a screw to keep the toe horizontal. Once the bone at the joint became fused, doctors removed the screw and gave it to me as a souvenir of my visit to Sunnybrook. The result of the doctors' handiwork has removed the flexibility of my left toe, but it is certainly something that I can live with.

When all of the repairs were completed to my ailing carcass at Sunnybrook, those in charge of my recovery discharged me by ambulance to the old Orangeville Hospital on First Street where I was to complete the remainder of my rehabilitation, before heading home.

Considering that the accident occurred on September 8, Halloween was the scary day that those in charge deemed me to be sufficiently recovered to be sent home. Dr. Walter Henderson, my attending physician in Orangeville, took me to a set of stairs at the hospital's main entrance and asked, "Can you climb those stairs?" I replied, "How high do you want me to go?" Since I was able to walk up to the landing and back down again, he made the decision to sign my release.

Due to the fact that our bedroom on Church Street was on the second floor accessible only by a steep set of stairs, Dorothy arranged for the loan of a cot which was placed in our living room until I was able to navigate my way upstairs. The cot was where I crashed out at night or whenever I needed a rest.

I was able to feed myself when I got home, but didn't object to Dorothy cutting up my food on occasion until I finally mastered the intricacies of using a knife and fork easily. As a result of my accident, I lost 40 pounds, or approximately one quarter of my weight. Once I got back to eating regularly,   I too often indulged in cream puffs and other deserts which have always been my weakness and soon regained my lost weight (and then some). Ever since, I've hoped to regain my pre-accident weight (an unlikely objective) but I continue to eat sensibly in the hopes of not ballooning beyond a respectable weight. 160 pounds I believe would be a great weight for me but I doubt I have the willpower to regain it again (but at least I will keep trying).

To build up my endurance and muscle strength, I arranged for the purchase of an exercise bicycle and light set of weights and once I was able to walk I enjoyed strolling around our block, listening to birds singing, as I regained my freedom.

Following the accident, my left side was left black-and-blue probably indicating nerve damage, which I believe lingers to this day. The fine motor nerves of my left hand still are not back to normal, but to help in their recovery, thirty–five years after the accident, I am attempting to master the five-string banjo. As my music instructor, Eric Nagler commented, "You may never be good enough to make it to Carnegie Hall, but as long as you are having fun, that's the most important thing!" I believe that I am making progress in my musical efforts, but more importantly I am activating a few unused brain cells in the process, and my left hand dexterity, is improving. I have also been able to dispel that old adage: "You can't teach an old dog new tricks!"

Once I had regained sufficient strength and dexterity, I had no trouble driving, but did encounter one unexpected problem. On a visit with Dorothy to the Orangeville Mall, we completed shopping inside then returned to our car in the parking lot. The only problem was, I had no idea where I'd parked the car in the lot! Following that event, I had to relearn to become more observant. From then on, whenever and wherever I parked, I had to take note of the exact location. This would be the usual practice for any normal person in such a parking situation. It was particularly important in a much larger lot, to select a nearby fixed object for reference because the vehicles around where I'd parked likely will have changed by the time I got back to the vehicle. A related, but slightly different problem happened when I drove in a strange town. Following a series of turns, left, right, right, left, etc., I found myself easily confused unless I kept careful track of my turns.

Approximately six months after my release from hospital, I received a call from Sunnybrook requesting my participation in a research study. I believe a project was being conducted by Sunnybrook medical students studying for their Masters degrees. They were examining how patients who'd suffered head injuries were coping after their release from hospital.

It turned out that some ex-patients became drug addicted, alcoholics, or ended with broken marriages when unable to cope. Those conducting the project gave me a series of tests and made suggestions as to how ex-head injury patients could cope with problems they might experience. I was pleased to discover that on my own, I had already been doing a lot of things which they suggested. This involved such activities as becoming more observant, writing notes to remind myself of events, and such other memory assists. It was heartening to realize that on my own I was already doing a lot of the right stuff.

Since I was back to full-time teaching one year after the accident, I became concerned with my voice. Due to my tracheotomy in Sunnybrook, I began to wonder if my speech had been affected. I didn't think that my diction was as good as it should be or that I could project my voice well enough to be heard clearly at the back of the classroom. To deal with these questions, I visited a local speech therapist, from whom I received a few vocal exercises which I could practice. I think that many of these concerns with my voice were unfounded but I figured that the voice exercises in any event would be of some value to me.

All in all, my determination to recover and common sense went a long way to taking some of the troublesome wrinkles out of my recovery process. Any shortcomings still in my performance three dozen years after the accident may be due to lingering effects of the accident or are more likely just part of the normal aging process which has been going on for in excess of three score and ten years.

Thinking back to the accident in 1979, I could have ended up much worse than I did. I might have ended up paralyzed, dead, or who knows in what other sorry condition. I guess that it just wasn't my time. I know that such thoughts have made me appreciate life more and it might explain why these days I go out of my way to do things for others (maybe it's just because I can). All of these recoveries from my accident have further reinforced my admiration for the resiliency of the human body and the mysteries of life in general.

2 Mind Over Matter

I believe that the mysteries of the human brain are vaster than those of outer space. The resilience of the human body continues to fascinate me, generating questions such as the following: While my wife Dorothy visited me regularly in Sunnybrook, was it possible that her concern exuded a form of energy which actually helped with my recovery? This same question would apply to anyone involved in their own healing experience. After the accident, folks asked, "What do you think, are you 85% of what you were before the accident, 70%, 90%, or what?" I began to wonder if my response maybe should be, "would you believe 110%?" Being forty years old at the time of the accident, I wonder what changes in my mental functions have taken place as a result of the accident and neurosurgeons poking and prodding into my little gray cells? Has the accident fractured and rerouted forty years of my brain's carefully crafted network? During an assessment following my treatment by Dr. Charles Tater of Sunnybrook, he referred to 'islands of memory.' I know that I have forgotten some past events completely, and a few activities are more difficult following the accident. Some experts believe that at the time of birth our brains are tabula rasa or blank slates and that all knowledge comes from experience and perception. If there ever was such a phenomenon as tabula rasa when I came into existence, then following my accident I would consider that my collision produced an example of tabula fractus. Some of my functions became less sharp, but I was still able to teach even complex mathematical lessons after the accident. Certain perception problems surfaced making it awkward to relate small textbooks to the large blackboard work, and I believe that my writing is worse, but it was never any hell, even at the best of times. In general, I feel that I've lost little as a result of the accident, although there are some subtle changes that even I probably don't realize. Am I a better person as a result of my new cranial rewiring? Experts have proven that when one loses a sense such as vision, other senses become heightened to compensate for any loss. Have I inherited insights which I never would have gained without the assistance of my neurological trauma? I'll probably never know for sure, but it will sure give me a few more questions to ponder. As a result of my cycling accident, I have not lost my sense of humour. Perhaps it has become a bit bent and more twisted, but it does remain intact. During my recovery in Sunnybrook, I can recall my attempts at frivolity (although feeble) however I'm not sure that hospital orderlies and nurses, or any of my visitors found my jokes based on being in hospital laughable. The following story is a fictional incident based on my stay in Sunnybrook.

Testing Nurse Florence Boyle's Patience

Clarence Fogarty hated the scrubbed sterile corridors, and the antiseptic smell of the hospital. They reminded him of death, but he had to admit that they were also signs he was still alive. As Clarence lay in his hospital bed with his bare posterior exposed for all the world to see, the sharp words of head nurse Florence Boyle commanded his attention. "Did you get that pill down your throat like I told you to?"

"Pill . . . for gawd's sake Florence, it's the size of a ten-pin bowling ball! How the Hell do you expect me to swallow that thing?"

"Quit complaining! It's all for your own good. Take a little sip of water, and it'll slide right down."

"Hardly likely! Besides I've heard that taking too many antibiotics like that might develop a superbug in me that becomes more resistant to the original drug."

Head nurse Boyle just continued to glare through her squinty eyes. "When did you get your medical degree that allows you to question the medical diagnosis and treatment of a specialist like Doctor Doolittle?"

"Dr. Doolittle! Now that's an apt name if I ever heard one! What does he know about what I can swallow? He's just getting back at me for calling him a quack when I was first admitted!"

"Listen you horrible little man! Your lousy attitude is getting tough for me to swallow as well! You realize of course that you're in the intensive care unit, and there are only two ways out, either, feet-first, or you walk out under your own steam. Your wife told me that you might be a difficult patient."

"My wife? What does she know? She's not here to see how my sweet and lovable nature is being tested by the medical staff of this hospital!"

"Sweet and lovable nature? You've got to be joking! I don't think you have a sweet or lovable bone in your whole body! I think they were all broken in your accident. If you don't soon start to do what you are told, you *will* be going out of here feet first."

"Feet first? Are you threatening me Nurse Boyle?"

"Threatening you? Keep up your complaining, and you'll be wearing this bedpan for a halo!"

Clarence smiled knowingly as he imagined Florence Boyle bouncing a bedpan off his skull. He decided that he'd better retreat and attempt to regain whatever compassion he could still suck up to. "Relax Florence, I was only kidding. You can even tell the good doctor that I never did think he was a quack, and that I'm getting really great care from you folks here in the ICU."

One final glance at Florence Boyle convinced Clarence that, "Hell hath no fury like an irate head nurse with a hypodermic in one hand and a suppository in the other."

Author Norman Cousins in his book *Anatomy of an Illness* discusses the effects of laughter to help him to recover from a crippling disease. Perhaps without me realizing it, humour was one of the factors which contributed to my speedy recovery. That's just one more of life's little mysteries upon which I might muse, but never be able to prove.

In addition to speculation on the effects of humour in aiding recovery from an illness, author, Norman Cousins also used a visit with cellist Pablo Casals to pose the possibility that creativity also had a profound effect on the human body's ability to survive and rebuild. Casals suffered from rheumatoid arthritis and emphysema which hampered his breathing and movement, but when he sat down at his cello, "He began to play, his fingers, hands, and arms were in sublime coordination as they responded to the demands of his brain for the controlled beauty of movement and tone. Any cellist thirty years his junior would have been proud to have such extraordinary physical command. A man almost ninety, beset with the infirmities of old age, was able to cast off his afflictions, at least temporarily, because he knew he had something of overriding importance to do. Creativity for Pablo Casals was the source of his own cortisone. It is doubtful whether any anti inflammatory medication he would have taken would have been as powerful or safe as the substance, produced by the interaction of his mind and body."

A visit as well to ninety year old Dr. Albert Schweitzer at his hospital in Lambarene reinforced Cousins' opinion that music revitalized the elderly doctor. After playing Bach's Tocca and Fugue in D Minor on his piano, "The effect of the music was much the same on Schweitzer as it had been on Casals. He felt restored, enhanced. When he stood up, there was no trace of a stoop. Music was his medicine, but not the only medicine. There was humour Albert Schweitzer employed humour as a form of equatorial therapy, a way of reducing the temperature and the humidity and the tensions. His use of humour in fact was so artistic that one had the feeling he almost regarded it as a musical instrument." Having read these two accounts in Norman Cousins' book, although I'm not an accomplished musician, I can't help but speculate that my hidden desire to be creative through writing, art and later the 5-string banjo, may have been added factors in my being "too stubborn to die" while a patient at Sunnybrook Hospital.

A drunk who staggered home on a dark night stumbling from one lamp post to the next, likely followed a more direct path than the meandering one I pursued towards a lifelong career in education. I spent fifty-one years, or approximately two-thirds of my present seventy-four, under the thumb of educational institutions, (eight years in primary school, five in secondary, four at university, and thirty-four as a high school teacher). None of what took place during these years was part of what Robbie Burns would call carefully laid plans of either mice or men!

I have been called artistic, eclectic, peripatetic, and even eccentric, but consider all of these terms to be complements. Any one of them is certainly better than being called boring. The operative word in my life is curiosity, and my aim always has been to seek the truth in its many changing forms, although the ultimate truth (whatever that may be) continues to escape my grasp. I view life as being filled with questions but few definitive answers.

I am not a sports star, rock star nor a Nobel prize-winner, or any similar celebrity. Why then would I consider writing my memoir? The answer is probably two fold. First, to quote James Thurber, "I don't know what I think, until I read what I have to say." The second reason: "everyone has a story, and I'd like to determine what mine actually is before I die. It will give me a chance to document my legacy and speculate on what I feel my life has been all about."

As a life-long seeker, my chief tool has been learning. The theme of this memoir examines learning as it has molded my life to date and how most of this learning was not obtained in the usual fashion in the traditional 'skules' that I attended.

Although my principal theme in this memoir is learning, humour has also woven an insidious thread through my life. I will allow my unbridled sense of humour to surface where it will throughout this document. Who knows? It might even make your reading more palatable?

3 An Illustrious Gene Pool

I do not believe the concept that at the time of my birth my mind was a tabula rasa or blank slate, rather human brains are pre-hardwired for functions such as speech and I support a quotation by theologian John Selby Spong. "I carry within myself, in ways that I cannot conceive, not only the heritage of the gene pool that created me, but also the cultural and emotional history that shaped me."

When John Richard Holden McCarthy met Helen May (Nell) Hurley at the Dalton harness racing track in Timmins in 1924, that event brought together two of the greatest family names in Irish History, the McCarthy and the Hurleys. Being descendants of Celts, the McCarthy and Hurley Celtic ancestors stripped before battle and fought while wearing only sandals and a golden necklace or torc. Brandishing sword and shield, the naked warriors advanced into battle screaming towards their terrified Roman adversaries. Following the blood-curdling skirl of pipes, my McCarthy-Hurley ancestors' charge into battle was an extravaganza exhibiting all of the terrors of Hell itself. Both family names, like the persona themselves, evolved over time through a series of permutations.

In its earliest form, Carthach means 'the loving one' while MacCarthy translates as 'the son of Carthach.' MacCarthys claim ancestry back to the third century to the reign of Oiloildum, King of Munster. Cormac, the son of King Oiloildum of Munster, later also became king. There appears to have been several Cormac MacCarthys in Irish history. Cormac Laidir (the strong) MacCarthy built Blarney castle. Cormac MacDermot MacCarthy fought against Queen Elizabeth and put off her demands for allegiance using 'soft speech intended to deceive.' His efforts led to the reputation of the Blarney stone becoming known to impart eloquence to those who kissed it.

MacDonagh MacCarthy Lord of Duhallow was one of the 'hard case' MacCarthys who built enormous castles by forcing passersby to work on these fortifications. After working them to death, MacDonagh had the dead labourers' blood mixed in with the castles' mortar. The McCarthy coat of arms is described as, "Argent a stag trippant attired and unguled or', which means 'A trotting red stag with horns and hooves of gold on a silver background.' The crest features, "a dexter arm in mail argent, holding in the hand a lizard both proper." That is, 'A right arm in blue armour from which the normally coloured hand holds a naturally coloured lizard.' The McCarthy motto: "Forti et fideli nihil difficile" translates as, "Nothing is difficult to the brave and faithful." The MacCarthy name dropped a few letters evolving through Macartney, MacCarthaigh, MacCarthy, McCartee, McCarthaigh, McCartie, McCartney, McCarty, until it finally became the McCarthy name of today.

Castlelough, now partially ruined, was one of the great, beautifully situated castles of McCarthy Mor. In 1214, a war broke out between two McCarthy kinsmen and Kerry became studded with Anglo Norman castles. It is thought that the castle on Lough Lein was built by the Roches.

In 1261, the McCarthys invaded Kerry from West Cork and killed Gerald Roche. Cormac McCarthy was himself slain and a cairn on Mangerton Mountain marks the spot where he fell.

Henceforth, the McCarthys ruled South Kerry from three castles at Castlelough, Pallas and Ballycarberry. The chief of the McCarthys was McCarthy Mor. In 1565, Queen Elizabeth granted Donald McCarthy Mor the title, 'Earl of Glencar'.

In 1588, the Earl of Glencar mortaged Castlelough to Florence McCarthy-Reag, who had married his daughter Ellen. In 1605, she obtained a portion of her father's lands, and her brother Donal was granted Castlelough and a 5000 acre estate. He is known in local tradition as, 'Dan the Feathers' since, as a brave warrior, he displayed a passion for securing as trophies the plumed helmets of Elizabeth's troops. He made such a sport of collecting plumes from these helmets that women were employed in his stronghold in the making of feather beds. He died quietly but not before the English Chivalry dubbed him, "the Robin of Munster."

Throughout history, mother's Hurley name evolved as the Gaelic Muirthile then O'Muirtile meaning 'descended from the son of Muirtile' which became Anglacized, as O'Muirhly, O'Hurley, and finally Hurley. 'Commane' was a bizarre spelling of Hurley which originated in County Clare when the name became erroneously translated from 'Caman,' the term referring to the stick used in the Irish game of hurley. The characters making up the Hurley line of evolution were as colourful (if not more so) than the MacCarthys. They included participants in the Crusades (earning them the motto Dextra cruce vincit, translated as, 'My right hand captures the cross'). Their blazon of arms features, "Argent, on a cross gules, five frets couped or" and the crest, "Out of an antique Irish crown or, a naked arm embowed proper, holding a crosslet." Hurley was a principal chief in Counties, Limerick, North Tipperary, and West Clare. They were a rich and powerful clan which constructed fortresses and churches which still remain standing in Ireland to this day. One important branch of the Hurleys settled on the Hill of Knocklong commanding a magnificient view of the Galtee Mountains and the plains of County Limmerick. This branch represented Killmalock in the parliament of 1505 and 1689.

One of the most remarkable characters in Ireland was the infamous Patrick Hurley of County Clare, the self-styled Count of Mountcallan. English officials captured the count after a long and spirited chase, and the adventurous and infamous career of Patrick Hurley ended in 1700 when officials tried, convicted, and hung him for being an informer.

English Protestants persecuted many of the Hurleys for their Catholic beliefs, and one of the most famous prelates of the first persecution era was Dermot O'Hurley Archbishop of Cashel. He is noted for his martyrdom when defiantly refusing to acknowledge the 'Queen's religion' in Ireland. Born in County Limmerick the Archbishop was educated in Paris and Louvain and in 1581 appointed to the See of Cashel. Soon after arriving at his post, he was arrested 'bearing treasonable papers' and subjected to torture. The persecutors placed the Archbishop's feet and calves in tin boots filled with oil. They then fastened his feet in a stock and built a fire under them. Boiling in oil, morsels of flesh fell from his feet and legs leaving them 'bare bone.' In spite of torture, the Archbishop refused to acknowledge the Queen's supremacy in matters of religion. His suffering ended when his enemies hung him from a tree outside Dublin. In 1586 the English also made a martyr of the Franciscan Brother Donagh O'Muirhily Bishop of Ross 1562-1570. His enemies incarcerated the bishop in the tower of London where he remained a prisoner for ten years until his death.

Oliver Cromwell was born into a common family of English country Puritans and at age 27 he felt seized by a sense of divine destiny. Historians described Cromwell as, "a country squire, a bronzed-faced, callous-handed man of property who worked his farm, preyed, fasted often, and spoke seldom." Cromwell attracted attention as justice of the peace when he had loafers collared in taverns and forced them to join in singing hymns. As self-proclaimed 'Lord Protector,' when Cromwelll stuck his long English nose, warts and all, into the hornets' nest of Irish Catholicism, he stirred up some irate Hurleys as enemies. I have not traced my family lineage precisely through my genealogical past, but it is difficult to believe that my genes have not been in the least affected by the potential illustrious gene pool of the McCarthy and Hurley characters that I have described.

Perhaps I have inherited within me a gene of a Crusader, or one from a king, an Archbishop, a Franciscan, or brigand count. I might even possess one from an owner of Blarney Castle, thus explaining my yen to yak and tell tales. Considering aspects of genetics and heredity, there is a chance that my being also contains at least a single cell from my great-great-grandfather Jeremiah D. McCarthy who emigrated from Wexford Ireland in the 1800's. Potential Hurley genes inherited from mother would have originated from her Irish roots. One or more cells may also have drifted into my persona from a young Canadian Metis maiden who by some misadventure crept through marriage into my mother's (black sheep) Hurley side of the family (as mother might have described it). Any other unknown or unusual genetic influences would certainly provide additional spice to my genealogical makeup. Traits inherited from such a potentially wide variety of donor ancestors such as the ones I've listed plus any hard-wired functions suggest to me that when my life began, my brain was not a tabula rasa or blank slate, but that my mind was off and running with an input of Irish blarney giving me a head start as soon as I popped into the world.

Mom & Dad

If there is any chance of inheriting genes or habits, the most logical donors would be my joint procreators, my dad John Richard Holden McCarthy, and my mom Helen May (Nell) Hurley. John Richard Holden was born March 4, 1898 in Mattawa, a town clinging like a leech to the south bank of the Ottawa River. His grandfather Jeremiah D. McCarthy hailed from Camolin, Wexford County Ireland, born perhaps 1787. After Jeremiah immigrated to Canada, the1851 census of Upper Canada lists his trade as a blacksmith; however, at the time of his death records report him as being a farmer. He was likely both. Rev. John Butler conducted Jeremiah's funeral July3, 1861, and oversaw his burial in St. Paul's Anglican cemetery in Fitzroy

Harbour on the shore of the Ottawa River. Jeremiah's age was 74 at the time of his death due to "inflammation of the prostate'.

My dad's family moved to Mount Nickel, 5 miles north of Sudbury, then to Timmins in 1916. In 1917, Holden enlisted in the army's Royal Hamilton Light Infantry. He spent time on the firing range in Aldershot, England. Holden was one of 12 recruits who made marksman and remained behind to try sniping tests, and thus become known as one of Currie's favourites. Many of his other buddies went off to war with the 102nd, while snipers went to the 58th Battalion, D Company, 13th Platoon.

Dad WWI

Following his release from the army, dad remained tight-lipped and was not one to speak about what could have been his horrific experiences during the war. I don't believe that he was not interested in reliving unpleasant memories, but in spite of what may have happened he re-enlisted joining the 22nd Infantry Reserves serving in the Second World War.

Following his military life, dad obtained a job as Front end Brakeman working for the Algoma Central Railway operating out of Sault Ste. Marie. Hands that once held a sniper's Lee Enfield rifle during the war were put to use swinging a railway lantern which controlled great steam locomotives, shunting box and flat cars through the freight yards and up through the Agawa Canyon. During blizzard conditions, I can picture him in the cab of a steam engine equipped with a plow as the monster engine lurched its way through mountainous snow drifts. While living in the Sault and working for the Algoma Central, Holden worked off and on at the McIntyre gold mine in Schumacher, balancing the uncertainty of work on the railway. Working in the McIntyre mill during the Depression Era he earned $4.00 for 8 hours work crushing and processing ore. In July 1924, at the Dalton Harness Horse Race Track in Timmins he met up with Helen May (Nell) Hurley, the only sure thing at the track that day. Holden likely didn't realize that day that his future father-in-law William Hurley, also known as Big Bill Hurley was one of the first pioneers in Algoma. United Church Pastor W.L.L. Lawrence married Holden and Helen September 15,1925 on the Hurley family farm. A write-up in the Sault Daily Star describes the ceremony. "Performed out-of-doors, the wedding party standing beneath a large maple tree which together with green vines and rose shrubs made a very effective background. After the ceremony, about 30 relatives and friends sat down with the young couple to enjoy a sumptuous repast, tables being spread upon the lawn and lighted by coloured lanterns strung above. The young couple were the recipients of many beautiful and useful gifts showing the high esteem in which they were held. Later in the evening they left for Sault Ste. Marie en route via Algoma Central Railway for Toronto, Niagara and other eastern points after which they will go to Timmins where they will temporarily reside. The bride travelled in a cocoa brown ensemble suit, trimmed with fur with shoes, gloves and hat to match."

The young couple was not long in beginning a family. During the four years from 1928 to 1932 inclusive, they produced five children Lola, Gerry, Eldon, Ruby, and Wayne. There followed a hiatus of two years when Vance was born on May 24,1934. After a five year breather, on April 19, 1939, I appeared on the scene. (Perhaps accidentally?)

4 Willie's World

McCarthy Family Left to Right: Wayne, Vance, Lola, Dad, Gerry, Mom, Ruby, Clare, Eldon

This was the world into which at 4:30 in the morning of Wednesday, April 19, 1939, midwife Mrs. Elsie Byron presided over my introduction as William Clare into the wonderful world of Gold Centre. As Wee Willie, I flexed my newfound vocal chords by uttering a screech at a level somewhere between that of a chainsaw running at full throttle and a howling pack of Huskies. Even though harbingers of spring had arrived, meteorological records reported a temperature hovering just below freezing, with half an inch of snow blanketing the northern landscape.

The William of 'William-Clare' was in honour of mom's father, William (Big Bill) Hurley who died the year of my birth, while the Clare is in memory of dad's deceased baby brother. That year was also the date of several technological advances. Julian S. Kahn received a patent for his invention of a can for dispensing substances under pressure. But I do not consider the invention of a can to dispense whipped cream or bug spray to be at the top of the list of the world's most significant scientific wonders. 1939 also marked the maiden flight of the first direct-lift helicopter. This event in history ironically was relevant to my survival when a helicopter 'Bandage One' saved my life following my bicycle accident in 1979. It was a helicopter which transported my crumpled carcass from Orangeville to Sunnybrook Hospital in Toronto. In 1939, a litre of milk sold for ten cents, the cost of a loaf of bread was nine cents, and a litre of gas a nickel. Hopefully my arrival on God's green earth could not be construed to be the cause of the start of the Second World War!

My first learning environment and perhaps the most significant one was the hamlet of Gold Centre where I was born. This tiny town tucked into the bosom of Northern Ontario perched like a contented bullfrog sitting on a granite rock in an evergreen pond of pine and spruce. Gold Centre was so small it contained only two fire hydrants, but no stop signs. Any household without a ready source of running water had to obtain it by running with a container to one of the hydrants for a fill which they would then have to lug home.

When our family migrated from Sault Ste. Marie to the Timmins area in the early 1930's, they settled temporarily in Schumacher on 1st Avenue, and in 1936 moved to #65, 2nd Avenue next door to future NHL hockey star Dean Prentice. One of these houses was actually a log cabin. The family finally came to rest in Gold Centre in a house purchased likely because it contained a vacant store which mother immediately commandeered. There was a cellar beneath the house, but no real basement per se. The cellar did contain the luxury of a spring fed well from which water could be pumped by hand. Since the cellar would often flood after spring thaw or heavy rain, an antiquated hand-operated boat's bilge pump in the cellar served as a sump pump. Boards surrounding the pump would on flood occasions float. Brothers Gerry and Eldon had the task of checking the bilge water and pump it out if necessary with a back-and-forth motion driving the water from the sump up outside to ground level.

In order to provide a proper basement, father used a horse and scoop to excavate out the ground beneath the house, then a poured foundation ensued. The boys helped dig septic lines and eventually running water and a proper bathroom became a reality. Prior to the construction of the new basement, toilet facilities consisted of a two-hole outdoor privy. The laneway leading past the back yard was a convenient route for a horse-drawn honey wagon to ply its trade during the summer. The contraption morphed into a sled to collect outhouse waste during the winter. Once indoor plumbing became available, ever-practical father converted the redundant privy into a storage shed. He attached coat hooks high on the walls to hang several bicycles by their front wheels. A Quebec heater in the living room provided heat for the pre-basement house. The heater's pipe pierced the attic where the kids slept. Heat radiating from the stove pipe provided the only warmth trickling in to the attic sleeping quarters. During the winter, frost was often visible on nails protruding through the ceiling. To tame the arctic attic air at night, kids usually slept with the morning's clothing tucked under the covers in bed with them. This made arising in the morning more comfortable, but in order to make their way into the kitchen for breakfast, the youngsters had to exit along a set of outside stairs then make their way back inside. Water for dishes and bath nights was obtained from the spring-fed well in the cellar and arrived via a hand pump on the kitchen sink.

The water was then heated in a reservoir on the end of the kitchen woodstove Once the new basement was completed, the sump pump was no longer necessary and father arranged for an octopus-like furnace to be installed. A chute built into the basement's front corner provided ready access for bags of coal to be dumped through a window and down into the wooden bin provided for coal storage. Since the kids were often sequestered in the attic, whenever mother wished to get their attention, she knocked on the kitchen ceiling with a broom handle. A song "Knock Three Times" became a popular song later. (A constant reminder of those early days as kids sleeping in the attic.)

Mother managed the house, and looked after her brood of seven children, and although she had her hands full tending to her household duties, she found time to open a general store in the space available in the house. Since this was the only store of any kind in town, there was no need to give it a name, it became known simply as 'the store.' Any advertising was due to common knowledge and word-of-mouth. Produce for sale on the shelves included canned vegetables and soups, while jars of candy and cones for ice cream lined the shelves, and items such as brown and white sugar, and oatmeal were displayed in bulk containers in front of the counter. Fresh vegetables were provided from our own garden behind the house, and neighbours gardens' surpluses. Frank Sattachi's farm less than a block from the store provided farm-fresh eggs, and anyone wishing a chicken for Sunday dinner, could obtain a Leghorn from Frank who would lop off the bird's head, but left the plucking and eviscerating to the buyer. Bread was not always available as one of the items for sale in the store, but if the need arose, mother might supply a loaf from her personal household stock, or else ask the customer to return after she'd baked additional loaves. Fresh milk was available in the store along with a variety of soft drinks supplied by McDonald's

Beverages in Timmins. During the winter it was common practice for the family's kids to collect icicles which had fallen from the eaves of the house. These chunks of ice tossed into the cooler eased the strain on the electrical supply needed to lower the temperature of the cooler. A freezer was used to store an ever-changing variety of pails of ice cream for hand-dipped cones. This ice cream was supplied by Eplette's dairy from Timmins. A pair of White Rose gas pumps stood majestically, just beyond the wooden sidewalk which ran parallel to the front of the store. Their tall glass cylinders were filled by means of hand pumps, and to dispense the fuel into a vehicle, a hose with nozzle and gravity feed did the job. Markings on the sides of the tall vertical glass cylinders determined the number of gallons of gasoline dispersed to a customer's vehicle.

Mother's store was the site of the only phone in the village, but anyone wishing to make a call or summon a taxi was free to enter through the store's front entrance then proceed to the wall phone in our living room. Several swift cranks would bring the operator onto the party line, and shortly thereafter, one of Dwyer's cabs from Schumacher would arrive to collect its passenger.

Mother knew everyone in town. The Halls were old folks who owned two Dalmatian dogs. I visited them often because Mrs. Hall always provided me with samples of her freshly baked cookies, while Old Mr. Hall would let me pet his pair of friendly mutts. Farmer Frank Sattachi lived just on the edge of town while Old Lady Coochmeister lived not far from Frank, on the last street in town. With a war in progress, kids used to throw stones at Missus Coochmeister's house just because she was German, then they'd run away. Brother Vance was one of those kids responsible for tossing a stone through Coochmeister's window and he no doubt received Hell from my parents who felt embarrassed and obligated to replace the broken pane. Westerholms lived down next to the tracks a block from the Greers who owned a team of Huskies. Whenever the old Ontario Northland steam engine 999 roared by on the tracks and the engineer blew the train's whistle, the Greer Huskies would howl. On the tracks was where we also placed pennies when we knew there was a train coming so the engine would flatten the coins which we used for decorations. The tracks were a natural extension to our Gold Centre world. We walked the tracks to Schumacher and used sling shots to fire rocks at insulators on the telegraph poles. Sometimes we found insulators intact, and would take them home as souvenirs. Brother Eldon once shot a Great-Horned Owl off the top of one of the telegraph poles. The bird fell to the ground, so Eldon shoved the owl under his coat to take the bird home to stuff. Mother made him leave the dead owl which turned out to be lousy in the front porch. After mother deloused Eldon, father deloused the house by igniting blocks of sulphur and placing the smouldering lice killers under the front porch.

The Ontario Northland tracks passing by Gold Centre also led to blueberry country. We knew that wherever there were blueberries, we'd usually find browsing black bears. While my father earned a living mining for gold in Schumacher's McIntyre Gold Mine, the rest of the family spent their time gathering blueberries, one of the other abundant assets of the North. The exact dates of blueberry season varied from year-to-year, but it was usually in July or August, that the kids in our family would set out with a collection of tins and baskets to pick berries. Magically, mother converted our pickings into pies, tarts, jams, and preserves. There was nothing like being drawn into her kitchen by the aroma or her baking blueberry pies, and sinking your teeth into a pie bursting with sweet juicy Northern Ontario wild blueberries.

We would reach our favourite site at the Seven Sisters outcroppings of granite, after trooping several miles down the

Ontario Northland railway tracks, then following hydro lines back
into the bush. It was not uncommon to be picking berries up the
side of one hill, while a family of bears did the same on an
adjacent slope. At some point, the munching bears would
collectively decide that the picking on our hill looked better than
theirs, so they would cross over to our hill, and we would then
cross over to the one vacated by the bears. The bruins might later
decide that their first hill, after all, was actually better than ours.
They would cross back to their original hill, and we would do
likewise. This hopping of kids and bears back and forth from hill
to hill would continue, until bears, pickers and the supply of
berries on all hills were exhausted.

On one berry picking expedition, my brothers Gerry and
Eldon spent the morning filling their containers, then decided to
pause for a short period of relaxation, playing at an abandoned
mine shaft and its related deserted buildings. The frolicking
youngsters left their pails of picked berries unattended on the
ground nearby. A passing bear discovered this unexpected bonanza,
and gobbled up the cache before continuing on its way. When the
lads discovered what had happened, they knew that if they returned
home empty-handed, their mother would send them out again that
same day, to refill their buckets. The truant pickers therefore
extended their play time, eventually arriving back home too late to
be sent back again that day to the Seven Sisters.

Large plump cultivated blueberries are usually available in
local grocery stores, but in no way compare with the smaller
flavour laden Northern Ontario variety. Science has proven that
blueberries' abundance of anti-oxidants makes them one of
nature's best health foods, and mother just naturally sensed this
and that picking berries in the wild was also an extremely healthy
and exhausting exercise for her brood of energetic kids.

As a young girl, my mother Nell Hurley gained her love of cooking from her mother Matilda on the family farm in Echo Bay. Nell's nostrils quivered as she inhaled the glorious aroma of baking bread in her mom's kitchen. She watched as her mother cut out biscuits to line up marching in rows down a cookie sheet. Nell waited for her mother to ask for help with the blueberry pie, the last item on the day's baking list. The Hurley family farm nibbled on the limits of the hamlet of Echo Bay, just a stone's throw south of Sault Ste. Marie. Nell was the second youngest of the family's dozen kids. Her favourite activity was sniffing the delightful kitchen aromas, and helping to supervise a variety of mysterious pots brewing on her mother's stove. In 1925 when Nell married and left home to raise her own brood of two girls and five boys, she brought her love of cooking along to her new relationship. I was the youngest member of the lot, and I still recall as a kid, the fond memories of the smells of baking bread, cookies, pies, and perhaps a roasting chicken. Before Tim Hortons ever dreamed of the Tim Bit, mother was in the habit of using donut holes to test the temperature of her cooking oil. She also created donut men with large heads and twisty arms and legs and her donut sinkers were always a family favourite, particularly at Christmas. Nell often put her cooking skills to good use at summer cadet Camp Bickel, and on occasion in the McIntyre arena's coffee shop.

Not all of her culinary experiments were successes however. Once while preparing grape jelly, she dangled a dripping cheesecloth sack of mushy grapes, over a bowl of accumulating juice on the kitchen table. When the string broke, the bag of mushy grapes plunked into the bowl of grape juice, and Nell instantly became the owner of the only wall-to-wall purple kitchen in the village of Gold Centre.

A Good Dose of Common Sense

A good dose of common sense was my mother's secret weapon for dealing with challenges in her life. She had no advanced academic or medical training but engaged life with her usual practical "grab the bull by the horns" approach.

Raising a family of seven kids forced her to dig deeply into her bag of survival tricks to cope with scarcities during the Great Depression and WWII rationing. Since our Northern Ontario village of Gold Centre was located several miles from any doctor, medical facility, or pharmacy, mother usually dealt with her tribe's assortment of scratches, scrapes, bruises, bumps and nauseas by applying her own personal brand of medical wisdom.

To help fortify us against Northern Ontario winters which frequently drove the mercury on our Fahrenheit thermometer, to a bone chilling minus fifty degrees, each fall she forced us to slurp down hefty doses of cod liver oil. Mustard plasters to relieve congested chests, and Mentholatum for clogged nostrils were two of her standbys. Good substantial meals were also a very important part of her daily regimen. Each morning during the winter, before she ushered us off to walk the two miles to school, we started each day with a stick-to-the-ribs breakfast of porridge chosen from her arsenal of oatmeal, Red River Cereal or Cream O' Wheat. Our house contained none of those wimpy, empty of nourishment sugarcoated, fruit loopy, snap crackle and pop, cereals which dominate the choice of today's breakfast cereals.

If a chicken was on the menu for the day, the carcass would always be used to brew her version of that powerful cure-all commonly known as chicken soup. When spring arrived, it was time for mother's tonic: a combination of brown sugar and turpentine. I believe the intent of this mysterious potent elixir was to clean-out and rid our systems of any lingering winter bacteria.

When brother Wayne sliced into his big toe with an axe while performing his wood chopping duties, mother didn't panic. She bathed and disinfected the wound before bandaging it, and followed with her usual dose of tender loving care. The only lingering effect of the incident is a minor scar to remind Wayne of that accident almost a half century ago. There was no Dr. Spock in those days telling parents how to raise their children, but I'm sure that mother could have written her own unique volume quite handily.

On several occasions after I had abandoned the family nest, rather than visit our local pharmacy, I resurrected her remedy for a scratchy throat: a mixture of butter and creamed honey with an added dollop of lemon juice. Northern Ontario is blueberry country and this marvelous fruit became our staple, both fresh and preserved throughout the year. Nutritionists only recently ascertained that blueberries' healthy properties are due largely to their high content of antioxidants. Mother and the black bears that roamed our favourite blueberry picking patches were both well aware of those benefits many years ago. Mother espoused the merits of hard work, good manners and compassion and passed these important traits along with her wonder medical cures to her offspring. She taught all of her children (including the boys) how to cook, a skill that most of us still use more than half a century later.

5 Kid Stuff

As a kid, there was no shortage of stuff to keep me busy in Gold Centre. The wooden sidewalk running the length of the road on our side of the street was an ideal drag strip for me to race my tin pedal car back and forth in front of the store and beyond. The open spaces between the boards created a rumble which in my mind sounded like a high speed racing car. To others it was just a rattling tinny racket. When I reached the age of five, mother enrolled me in Schumacher Public School. It was then up to me to make the two mile trek with my brothers and sisters to my first organized font of learning. Details of this time in life are scant in the cobwebs of my mind, either because I was young or else unimpressed with school. One of the few memorable events surrounding my enrollment that I recall was related to the fact that I bawled my head off not wanting to go to school. I much preferred to stay in Gold Centre and watch workmen constructing an asphalt sidewalk along the opposite side of our street. In the end, mother's not so gentle persuasion convinced me to attend that kindergarden version of an institute of higher learning. Thinking back to early events in my life, one memorable one that often comes to mind was the time I was playing outside and had to go to the bathroom. Arriving at our front door, I pounded and hollered to be let in. The final result was the fact that I wet my pants on the doorstep. I'm not sure of my age at the time, but whatever it was, I couldn't quite reach the door knob.

During the winter it was not unusual for the temperature to drop to more than forty degrees Fahrenheit below zero. Eldon recalls the day that the mercury dropped to about minus fifty degrees. Walking on snow that cold, he said that it crunched underfoot and it was almost like walking on broken glass. Even though it was usually very cold, one saving grace was the fact that it was a dry crisp cold. Muffled in woolen toques, scarves, mitts and sweaters, my cheeks glowed a rosy red and the moisture from my breath formed a cloud in the frigid air. In hindsight, I believe that it was one of the healthiest times of my life. It was likely too damned cold for any insidious bacteria to hang around. This was the time of year when our sleds, toboggans, and skis got a good workout on the hills at the edge of town. My brothers and sisters would ski down hills and zip up across the railway tracks where Old Ontario Northland steam engine 999 was one of hazards of such a maneuver. I usually restricted my involvement to sleds and toboggans, building snow forts, and pitching snow balls instead. The nearby bush was an ideal spot to try out snowshoes and go on Christmas tree hunts when that festive time of year arrived. Father and the boys would set out in search of the ideal Christmas tree. Father usually selected a prime specimen larger than necessary but with a perfect top. Once the tree was cut down and lugged home on a toboggan, he would manicure the top to fit our living room and use excess boughs for additional decorations. What could smell more festive than the aroma of pine needles, accompanied by the odour of roasting turkey in the oven? Since father was one of the workers at the McIntyre Gold Mime in Schumacher, he received a turkey as a gift each year at Christmas. On one occasion he brought home a goose instead, but mother said it was too greasy cautioning him not to ever repeat such a choice. Christmas decorations were usually made with strings of pop corn, pine cones and an angel for the top plus whatever other decorations we could construct. Mother ran strings across the living room and used these to display the Christmas cards received that year. Most gifts were handmade including essentials such as woolen scarves, mitts, toques, gloves, and sweaters. Since this was during the depression, we never had much money to spend on gifts. For each kid's gift, it was traditional for us to receive a giant cardboard box packed with newspapers but containing one cherished food item hidden somewhere inside. It might be a jar of peanut butter, block of Kraft cheese, bottle of catsup, chunk of bologna or whatever edible item that person preferred. Although there was little cash to provide expensive gifts, we had another source to which we looked forward. Frederick Schumacher was an American investor and mining magnate after whom the town of Schumacher was named. Each year at Christmas he would take on the role of Santa Claus. At school just before Christmas, lists posted in schools itemized the gifts available from which students could make a choice. Gifts ranged through sleds, wagons, skis, skates, toboggans, dolls, books, toy sewing machines, etc. Teachers received gifts such as books, ties, gloves and various other forms of apparel. In addition to a gift, each student received a jar of hard rock candy. When Schumacher died, his estate continued the Christmas gift giving tradition thus extending the practice for a total of approximately three quarters of a century. In Northern Ontario at that time, there definitely was a Santa Claus. I still possess a Walt Disney book entitled 'The Cold-Blooded Penguin' that I received as a kid from Mr. Schumacher.

Our usual Christmas turkey was accompanied with mother's homemade pies, cookies, and her specialty, donuts. Although we had little cash to spare at Christmas, there was always an abundance of good cheer as the kids played games of snakes and ladders or Monopoly, then skied, or tobogganed or went for a skate on an outdoor pond to play hockey. Bundled up for the winter winds and arctic temperatures, we were usually too busy enjoying the winter to notice the biting cold.

In approximately 1944, our ever-on-the-move family

moved several blocks from the storehouse to Westerholms apartment building. Due to the size of our family (9), we actually took over two apartments in the new location. Father removed a wall separating the two apartments making them into a single large one. My memories of that location was the long set of wooden stairs leading up to our apartment on the second floor. Salient memories that linger include a sand pile beneath the stairs where I often played with toy vehicles, stones, chunks of wood, and a lot of imagination. I still cherish memories of mother working in the kitchen as she baked bread, pies, donuts, and other tasty treats. A flour covered apron seems to have been her usual apparel, even when she hung the laundry out on the clothesline. A memorable event included brother, Vance in his bare feet stepping on a rusty nail, causing mother to work her emergency medical magic providing all of the TLC necessary to heal the wound. It was while we lived in the apartment building that a travelling photographer took my photo while I sat mounted astride his pony. I was probably 6-7 years old at the time. Perhaps that photo was one of the first indications that my life would continue as a peripatetic one. As this memoir is one of learning, hours spent playing in the sand under the stairs no doubt was a learning time when my imagination was stretched to its limit. The following radio story is also about putting my imagination to good use while listening to my favourite programs.

6 Remembering Radio

Do you remember listening to The Jack Benny Show, Fibber McGee and Molly, The Great Gildersleeve, The Life of Riley, or Amos N' Andy on the radio during the 1940's? Those were the days before transistors, stereo sound systems, DVDs, and wall-size flat screen TVs. When I was a kid during that era, our sole electronic entertainment was an upright Stromberg-Carlson radio. Standing on my tip toes, I could just reach the top of its ornate wooden cabinet perched on four stubby carved legs. A set of doors opened to reveal volume controls and tuning knobs to select the appropriate station on the am dial. The innards of the cabinet contained a collection of vacuum tubes, capacitors and other not very sophisticated electronic ware.

On Saturday evenings, it was traditional for my dad and his five sons to huddle around the set as the winds whipping down from the north stirred drifts of snow banked around our home. Father tuned in that night's NHL hockey game with play-by-play commentator Foster Hewitt. We awaited Foster's excited, "He shoots-he scores!" as another goal drifted into the net. Those were the days with the original six teams, Toronto, Montreal, Chicago, New York, Boston, and Detroit from which names such as Richard, Plante, Duff, Kelly, Broda, Lindsey, Horton, Howe, Syl Apps, and Frank Mahovlich coursed through the airways. We enjoyed the experience more, because many of these stars had begun their careers by playing in our local leagues. It was an era when the Leafs consistently won games and players were more interested in finesse and skill rather than fat contracts, finances, and endorsements.

Along with news and hockey, the radio provided the whole family with entertainment featuring such shows as, The Happy Gang, The Bickersons, and The Aldrich Family. Comedy shows included, Fred Allen, Jimmy Durante, Bob Hope, Red Skelton, Milton Berle, and ventriloquist Edgar Bergen with puppets Charlie McCarthy and Mortimer Snerd. As a kid, I was most interested in action programs such as Hopalong Cassidy, Sergeant Preston of the Yukon, and The Lone Ranger astride his great horse Silver and accompanied by his faithful companion Tonto. If your bent leaned more towards mysteries, you could tune in detective stories featuring Sam Spade, Boston Blackie, Philip Marlow, Michael Shayne, The Saint, This Is Your F.B.I., or Dragnet. Thrillers included The Inner Sanctum (with its creaking door), The Whistler and The Shadow, or for a change of pace, Songs by Sinatra, or Hawaii Calls, with host Webley Edwards broadcasting from the beach at Waikiki.

By comparison, it is impossible these days to experience a TV program without being overwhelmed with explosions, and battles, enhanced by million-dollar special effects, but very little story. Many North American shows such as the CSI series focus on blood and gore based on little mystery or substance. Readers would be wrong to assume that the radio shows of the 40's were boring without the glitz of today's media enhancements. It is my opinion that a major feature of old radio programs was that they consistently invoked a listener's imagination. The quality of stories told over the radio I believe were superior to many hollow current episodes. Having recently dug out from my dusty collection of old stuff, a set of twenty cassettes featuring thirty hours of old time radio shows, I was intrigued by the commercials featured half a century ago. Maxwell House Coffee was good to the very last drop, while Chesterfield, Camels, and Philip Morris cigarettes avoided the negative aspects of their products, stressing great tastes or the fact that doctors preferred these types of smokes.

Many old radio programs such as the Lone Ranger, Hopalong Cassidy, The Cisco Kid, Gunsmoke, and The Green Hornet have become television series, but in spite of producers' efforts, they are not as good as those generated by my young fertile imagination. Looking over my list of radio programs that existed over fifty years ago, there still exists a gold mine of possible characters that would provide fascinating series for television today, even if they didn't quite match up to my childhood imagination. If schools wished to promote a course on being creative and imaginative, there would be no better learning resource than to have students listen to a selection of old time radio shows. Students might even discover that the learning process can actually be fun!

Mother was always the organizer. This included a Halloween wiener roast at the sand pit on the edge of town. I suspect that this structured activity was meant to curtail the town lad's usual pranks of tipping over as many of the town's shit houses that they could.

In 1946 the war ended as did our life in Gold Centre. From our digs in the village, members of our family had been visiting Schumacher on a regular basis for school, church, work and recreation. Our new home in Schumacher, a two-story wood frame dwelling at 122 First Avenue was now only blocks rather than miles away from many favourite activities. My bedroom on the back of the house faced an alley way which ran parallel to the street in front of the house. A tin single car garage accessible from the lane way was used as storage for bicycles and other stuff, since we never owned an automobile. There was sufficient space in the back yard for dad to carefully pile rows of slab wood for our dwelling's space heater. I slept on the upper level of a bunk bed, and recall once falling out of the top bunk onto the floor while asleep. The family thought that the thud from my falling carcass when it hit the floor was made by a passing vehicle that had crashed into the house. Since a porch roof extended outward from the rear of the house, just below my bedroom window, I can recall on occasion climbing out at night onto the porch roof, an ideal spot from which I could view falling stars and other celestial events.

Our new house was approximately one block from a small grocery store accessible by rambling up the back lane while school was another 3-4 blocks beyond the store. More importantly, the next street over which ran parallel to the lane way fronted along a steep bank which in the winter became the location for many sliding events. With toboggans, sleds, or flattened cardboard boxes we would slide down the snow covered bank and across the roadway. First Avenue in front of our new house was the main route leading into Schumacher from Southern Ontario. If I hung a left upon reaching our back lane, the first street encountered was near the base of a steep hill. One of our idiotic pranks was to roll old used car tires from the top of the hill down towards First Avenue. By the time the rolling rubber reached the bottom of the hill at First, it had gained an incredible speed. It's a wonder there was never a serious collision between flying tires and frequent traffic approaching town.

On any streets during the winter, a favourite practice was to hunker down by stop signs waiting for automobiles to pass. We would then slink out, grab the car's bumper for a ride along the street behind a car as it gained speed. On occasion, there would be too many bodies clinging to the bumper, with the result, the car would be unable to gain traction. We would then drop off, and grab onto the bumper once the vehicle got moving again.

My learning reached a slightly different twist on one occasion when I was in grade four at Schumacher Public School where one class was taught by a teacher with a wooden leg. I assume that the man (a shop teacher) had an artificial leg as a result of a war injury or industrial accident. During one class, he was standing at the back of the room and asked, "What time is it?" Since I sat in the front row, I assumed that his question was directed at me sitting just under the clock. I was spared the embarrassment of answering when a fellow student blurted out the answer. This was lucky for me since I was unable to answer the question. What the incident did achieve, was to send me home that day determined to learn how to tell the correct time. Brothers and sisters took me aside and explained about significance of the big and little hands, teaching me to the point that I learned to tell time properly.

Our family attended the United Church two blocks from our First Avenue home and it was here that I fulfilled my religious obligations by attending Sunday school. My chief memory of this time of my life is based on a cartoon which I drew in one class. It was drawn in crayon on a chunk of newsprint. The image based on Genesis 28:10-19, to be exact. "And Jacob went out from Beersheba, and went toward Haran. And he lighted upon a certain place, and tarried there all night, because the sun was set; and took of the stones of that place, and put them for his pillows, and lay down in that place to sleep. And he dreamed, and behold a ladder set up on the earth, and the top of it reached to heaven: and behold the angels of God were ascending and descending on it." My cartoon depicted Jacob lying on the ground with his head resting on a rock. The drawing featured a golden ladder decorated in Jacob's dream by angels skipping with tiny wings up and down the ladder. Since I never got fried to a crisp by a bolt of lightning shooting down from heaven, for this sacrilegious depiction, I considered this granted me permission to produce editorial cartoons commenting on life, something I've doing for almost three-quarters of a century.

I do not recall any united Church minister to be memorable, but between our house and our church, there was a Roman Catholic Basilica presided over by a priest, Father Les Costello. The following two short stories document the colourful life of the famous man.

Father and I on step in Gold Centre

7 A Maverick Both Profane And Profound

Father Les Costello was a man, both profane and profound. Les could swear a blue streak, loved card-playing, gambling, a good cigar, a stiff drink of rye, and was a rabble-rouser who followed Christ. In order to profile Father Costello's life, it is best that I start at the beginning.

On February 16, 1928, a tiny baby bounced kicking and screaming into the lives of father, Jack and mother, Clare Costello. Their second child, Leslie John Thomas Costello swelled a complement that eventually grew to five children in a working-class Irish Canadian Catholic family. The church was of profound importance to the Costellos but their central focus was always, the kitchen table. Les grew up loving the gatherings of storytellers, and singers hovering around that entertaining spot. These gatherings nourished the distinctive mark of the Irish, with their magnificent breadth of spirit. No death could be properly mourned unless the halls rang with laughter. The Costello's world was still in the earliest days of radio. Les was a hyper kid with boundless energy who without sports would have driven everyone nuts. While he was growing up in his birth town of South Porcupine, in Northern Ontario, that time was the beginning of a hockey era. Kids' hockey games started when ice froze in November and carried on until the final slushy thaw in May. The lads played on streets, shovelled-out spots on frozen lakes, and on open air rinks set up with makeshift boards. They showed up in creative goalie pads, taped-together sticks, with Eatons' catalogues for shin pads, and frozen horse turds for pucks. Such games launched the careers of hockey greats the likes of Syl Apps, Frank Mahovlich, Tim

Horton, Dave Keon, Ted Lindsay, Gus Mortson, Bill Barilko, Gary Cheevers, Howie Meeker, and the Hannigan brothers Pat, Gord (Hopalong) and Ray. Les was a tough northern player who was a natural leader, and in many cases ringleader. Les's hockey career was sporadic until he joined the Holman Pluggers, his first organized team. Any worker who was also a good hockey player, was sure to be able to obtain a job at one of the gold mines, many of which had their own hockey teams, for which they were always seeking accomplished recruits. This was the starting place for the careers of many of the NHL's blossoming stars.

    Les Costello was saved from becoming a troublemaker by embracing academia. His high marks surprised those who noticed that he didn't spend much time on homework. Les had a fantastic memory, and a love of writing poetry composed of simple rhyming, in the style of Robert Service. His poems were usually about local characters such as Ozzie Bowes who ran the local rink. Les was a small hockey player who left many gouges on opposing players. His presence on ice was like 'a ricocheting cue ball on a snooker table.' He was seldom body-checked due to his shifty evasive style of skating. Les shouldn't be described as dirty, just tough. If Gordie Howe was known as 'Mr. Elbows' in the corners, I'm sure that even he could have learned a few tricks from watching Les Costello. Les left his home turf of South Porcupine to continue his schooling in grade 11 at St. Michaels in Toronto. Since St. Mike's actually served as a farm team for underaged players for the Toronto Maple Leafs, Les Costello's hockey skill eventually earned him a tryout with the Leafs. Since Les had little respect for rules and officialdom, his brash manner soon got him into the bad books of Leaf owner Conn Smythe. Smythe demoted Les to Pittsburgh, but Les was such an asset to that team, he was soon called up again to play for the Leafs. At the age of twenty, in 1948, Les Costello was a key member of the Leaf team when it won the Stanley Cup. Les was not interested in the notoriety of being a star NHL player, rather he simply enjoyed the challenge of the game. A turning- point came in Les's life after a Leaf defeat. He was whistling in the shower when a senior team mate advised him, "Hey rookie, there'll be no whistling after a team loss, or you'll be dead meat." This comment helped Les to make his decision to abandon his hockey career. One other display showing his lack of interest in being important occurred when the engraver for the Stanley cup asked him, "What name do you want placed on the cup for you?" Les replied, "Lester" rather than giving his true name Leslie. In response his mother's question, "Why did you tell him that?" Les answered, "It seemed like a good thing to do at the time." It was soon thereafter that he entered the seminary to become a Catholic priest.

God Loves the Rebel

On May 31, 1957, Les Costello turned his back on a promising professional hockey career when he was ordained, Father Leslie Costello, at St. Joachim's parish South Porcupine, in Northern Ontario. This prepared him to embark upon his true passion, helping the poor in a changing world. One of Father Costello's earliest churches was St. Alphonsus in Schumacher, where he fired off sermons with machine gun speed, fast punchy, and straight to the point, much like the way he talked. Father Les, or 'Cossie' as he was known by his pals, began each sermon with a joke, thereby grabbing the attention of his congregation, not wanting to miss the punch-line or any unexpected 'zingers.' Costello's earlier experience as a Toronto Maple Leaf player added to his appeal with the younger generation. When he wasn't on church business, 'Cossie' was down at the McIntyre Arena playing a pickup game with one of the mine's hockey teams, or encouraging both Catholic and Protestant kids to get out on the ice and play. Even though he was an ex-professional player, he never forgot the beauty of pond shinny where every kid had an equal chance to shine, and where fun was more important than victory.

Due to the tough lives of miners, Father Costello was frequently sought out for help. With no soup kitchens, food banks or other programs to assist the down-and-out, the rectory door became the number one choice for any folks in trouble. The yard in front of the church looked like a perpetual lawn sale. The rectory was overrun with used clothing, food parcels and furniture. When the choir came in to practice, it wasn't unusual to find a drunk sleeping behind the organ. On one occasion, when the driveway was littered with appliances, a parishioner was combing through the items. Father Les unleashed a withering barrage of four-lettered expletives that almost blistered the paint off St. Alphonsus. "Get away from those appliances! I just gave you a stove last week!" Les was never overly concerned about his own personal manner of dress. On occasion he would ride bare-chested on his bicycle through the streets of Schumacher. This was the way he went about his rounds visiting the sick and elderly. Coming up to Mrs. Dorothy McCarry's house, he'd pull out a ripped T-shirt from his carrying bag saying, "I'd better put this on, or Old Dorothy will be on my case!" His approach to funerals was a blend, of the sacramental tempered with Irish wit and irreverence. Les was always athletic. He biked and played tennis in the summer while in the winter he skied and played hockey, on a local old-timers team. Although always busy, he realized that there were many talented Catholic priest hockey players in Ontario. In 1962 he gathered enough players to form a team, to be called, 'The Flying Fathers,' which played its first game in North Bay in 1963. Although the players were talented and seldom lost a game, their focus was on slapstick entertainment. The team was comparable to the Harlem Globetrotters with Roman collars on ice. Costello was the biggest clown on the team. During a game, there might be an announcement over the PA system, "Father Costello, your wife wants you to call home. The baby's sick." As a result of their antics the team earned in excess of four million dollars for charity.

In addition to his other sporting interests, 'Cossie' loved to hunt and fish, a time when he could enjoy the solitude of the bush. It was freezing in early May when he headed out, too impatient to wait for a hunting buddy. He shot and bagged a partridge, but then while crossing a beaver dam slipped and fell, losing one of his boots in the muskeg. With one foot exposed, Les shoved it inside the still warm bagged partridge. Becoming disoriented, he wandered in circles until exhausted. As it became dark he curled up beside a tree where to keep up his strength, he ate cold the partridge he'd shot. Les prayed, and in the morning responded to a distant gunshot by firing his own rifle which alerted an OPP search party. Les's frost bitten hands and feet were not dealt with properly by his rescuers, and as a result doctors were later forced to amputate seven of his toes. The chances of Les ever being able to skate again were slim. However, he persevered to recover his sense of balance by skating for hours alone in the early morning darkness of the McIntyre arena. The number of Les Costello stories seems almost endless. They include the tale of the armless bell-ringer, the priest who showered while wearing his underwear. (He said he didn't like looking down on the unemployed) and the time he presented a hockey stick to Pope Paul VI in the Vatican, cautioning His Holiness how to hold the stick, "or they'll think you're stirring spaghetti." In 2002, during a pre-game practice with the Flying Fathers in Kincardine, Les who was still having problems with his balance, at the age of 74 fell, struck his head, and died from complications.

Father Costello's funeral was held in St. Alphonsus Church where his body lay in an open coffin flanked by an OPP honour guard for two nights. One of his fellow priests looking down at 'Cossie' in the coffin remarked, "God Bless, it's the first time I've seen him quiet." As the coffin was closed and prepared for transport to the McIntyre arena where two thousand mourners waited, Rev. Quinn, a Flying Father goalie gave the coffin a farewell knock in the same way Costello used to encourage friends and parishioners with a cheerful pat on the back. Father Les Costello was one of Northern Ontario's most colourful characters, epitomized by his favourite saying, "God loves the rebel."

My brother Eldon had the good fortune to work with Les Costello during a summer in the McIntyre Park, just before Les began his studies in the ministry. Eldon recalls Les as being a practical joker and prankster as he operated one of the park's grass cutting machines. Len Johnson of Orillia also played hockey in his younger days with Les at St. Michael's College in Toronto.

The McIntyre Community Building was a chief focal point for entertainment in Schumacher. Affectionately known as 'The Mac', the $200,000 structure was built for the exclusive enjoyment of McIntyre employees and their families. The facility seated 1,850 and was patterned after Maple Leaf Gardens in Toronto. It contained the ice rink with seating along the sides and a balcony at the end. The complex also contained a curling rink with adjoining coffee shop, bowling alley, gymnasium with basketball court where The Harlem Globetrotters once played. Beneath the ice rink's seating were lockers, team dressing rooms, and miniature ice surfaces in rooms where figure skaters such as champion Barbara Ann Scott practised. Mirrored walls of the practice rooms allowed skaters to check their form.

For hockey games I can recall hiding in lockers and niches below the stands before a game. We would then surface like rats once the game began. It was always a routine for arena staff to comb the area where we were hiding and boot out whoever they found. I think that often employees knew where we were hiding and simply cast a blind eye to us.

Boys in our family worked as rink rats cleaning ice surfaces with scrapers, brooms and shovels during hockey games and ice-capades. Those were the days before mechanized zambonis. The ancient zamboni's function was accomplished by two arena employees tugging a barrel mounted on two rubber tires around the ice surface. A wide mop dragged behind the barrel flooded the ice as water from the barrel poured out onto the dragging mop.

A cigar-smoking character Miro Guacci operated a skate sharpening business in a room in the complex. Besides sharpening skates, Miro was also paid to make ice, paint ice, surface the ice and play recorded music from the gondola like the one used by Foster Hewitt when he broadcasted games in Toronto.

The superb hockey facilities at the 'Mac' were used by the Schumacher Public School hockey team, and also led to the development of future NHL players such as Frank Mahovlich and his brother Pete, and the Hannigan boys, Gord, Pat and Ray. Most mines in the area had their own hockey teams, some of whom were paid professionals. These mine teams included names such as the Hollinger Green Shirts, the McIntyre Macmen, Pamour Dynamites, Coniaurum Flyers, Dome Porkies and Buffalo Ankerite Bisons. A famous line brought in by the Macmen was "The Coloured Line," Ozzie Carnegie, Herbie Carnegie and Manny McIntyre. These players who were all black were excellent players but were never accepted into the NHL because of their colour.

Since father worked at the McIntyre Mine, he would often spend his leisure time either watching or participating in curling. This was before and after his shift work. I can recall surprising him lounging watching a game of curling while he smoked a cigarette.

He immediately butted out the smoke or held it out of sight not wishing to influence us kids to mirror his smoking habit (he obviously smoked when he was alone) and he also enjoyed a glass of beer on the sly as well.

Activities which I fondly remember being held in the McIntyre complex include major circus attractions such as Ringling Brothers Barnum and Bailey. Wild performing cats were kept in wheeled cages at the outside of the arena near the back of the building before shows, and elephants and horses were tethered

outside on the grass. Such circuses with animal acts, aerial artists and clowns were fondest memories of my young life. The arena was once used by a Roy Rogers rodeo and on other occasions for bone-crunching wrestling matches featuring the likes of Whipper-Billy Watson, Pat Flanagan, Haystack Calhoon and The Shiek.

In addition to the community building, the McIntyre also groomed an extensive park system containing flowers, trees, shrubs and acres of grass. There was a play area for kids, a baseball diamond and a swimming pool on the way to Timmins.

A few Schumacher businesses included Bonfacio's Shoe Repair, Grant's Hardware, Gaye's Confectionary and Pulez's corner store where for a nickel, you could buy two cigarettes.

Back lanes were for garbage storage, but an enterprising kid could find brown Javex bottles, clean them up and turn them in to grocery stores for one cent refund. This cash might then be accumulated for the purchase of a theatre ticket, or a few cigarettes. As a kid living in Schumacher, I recall First Avenue, the main downtown street where Dwyer's Taxi was located, as was Anderson Photo Studio where our family photo was taken. There was also a bakery which sold scrumptious honey-dipped donuts and nearby was an ice cream parlour that we frequented when we had the cash. Miners of Schumacher were well situated to quench their thirsts. The town contained approximately fourteen hotels, (many of which were located on First Avenue) each of which operated its own beverage room. These watering holes provided workers with ample opportunities to obtain alcoholic brews. These were all without even considering the many local bootleggers!

8 On the Move Again

Left to Right:
Wayne, Vance, Ruby, Eldon,
Mom, Gerry, Dad, Clare, Lola

In 1948, our tribe was on the move again. While father worked in the McIntyre Mine, mother lived with fears of mine cave-ins and an assortment of other mine accidents and disasters. I suspect that this was one of her key reasons for initiating the move south. The other suspicion that I also have is that mother felt that there would be more and better chances for her seven children to have increased opportunities for jobs and education down in Southern Ontario. Remaining in Schumacher, where jobs were limited, her lads might end up working in the mines with their assorted perils. Once again, without knowing all the facts, I believe that mother was the spark plug behind this move and think that father was wise enough to go along with her suggestions. Having been married for approximately a quarter of a century, I'm sure that dad had learned to respect his spouse's wisdom.

To this end, mother headed south (probably by train) and met with her niece Marjorie Warrener in Stoney Creek. The two travelled to various spots in the Niagara Peninsula, and in the end mother agreed to purchase a two-story insulbrick house on an acre of land at 703 John Street in Dunnville situated on the Grand River, approximately five miles from its mouth on Lake Erie. Mother no doubt visualized that much of the acre would be suitable for a vegetable garden. In addition to the house there was a garage which could be used for storage since the family still didn't own an automobile. An added bonus of the property was a large number and variety of fruit trees, which included plum, apple, peach and pear.

When the time came to move, Wayne came down several days early, and slept in a sleeping bag on the floor of the new dwelling. Father rented a stake truck and its driver to transport the family belongings south, a distance of approximately 500 miles. The truck was overloaded and resembled the vehicle of TV's 'the Beverly Hillbillies.' The heavy load caused the truck's front end to rise and shimmy whenever they hit a bump. The rest of the family made the trip down by train to Hamilton from which Dick and Marjorie Warener transported them to the new digs in Dunnville.

It did not take long for mother to begin to cultivate the purchased chunk of land. Crops included potatoes, tomatoes, raspberries, strawberries and most other garden vegetables such as onions, radishes and cucumbers. One of my jobs as a kid was to peddle fresh vegetables for sale wherever I could in Dunnville.

Father obtained a job working at Lundy Fence Company as a general labourer, and later moved to Dominion Fabrics where he worked in the dye house. It was here that his work exposed him to caustic fumes from steaming vats of dyes, which aggravated emphysema which was originally brought on while working in the mines. Gerry worked as a machinist at Lundys, while Eldon took a job first at the Dunnville Dairy then at John S. Brooks Fishnet Company, earning him the nickname 'Fishie.' Ruby and mother both obtained jobs working in the office of The Monarch Knitting Mill.

I registered as a student in grade 5 at Dunnville Public School, graduating three years later to Dunnville High School. It was in the elementary school system that I can first recall an instance when I was the one to express an opinion shared by friends. I thus singled out myself to be the spokesperson for others. The incident in question concerned the school choir which was practising for the Christmas concert. Our music teacher was Miss Florence Kinard. Florence was working with a group consisting of me and some of my fellow male students. There was a lot of carping in our group, out of the ear shot of 'Flossie' Kinard that we didn't want to be singing in the school concert. During one practice in class, I had the gall to confess to Florence that I didn't want to participate in the concert. She went ballistic, tearing a strip off me for not wishing to contribute to the class project. When she said, "Is there anyone else who doesn't want to be in the concert either?" you could have cut the silence with a knife! Not one of my wimpy friends had the nerve to back out after the going over that I got. One would think that incident taught me a lesson, but I must confess that being a spokesperson for others got me into trouble more than once in my life later on.

During my elementary school life, my chief creative experiences involved drawings on coloured murals of classroom bulletin boards. Our grade 8 teacher was the school principal Alf Casselman who had the habit of leaving us supposedly unsupervised in the room. He would peer through the crack near the door's hinges spying on us to make sure that we were not up to any devilment while he was gone. In our eyes, we thought that he looked the complete ass for such antics. On the other hand, we students thought very highly of a young athletic male teacher, named Don Vale who played hockey on the town team.

At home, I did my share of work in the garden, pulling weeds, hoeing potatoes etc., while father was pressed into service operating a single-wheeled cultivator to work up the soil. When we arrived in Dunnville, not one to miss an opportunity, mother commandeered the garage to store bales of hay and chicken feed. She convinced father to build a hen house, then she purchased a brooder, and day-old chicks from the local hatchery. These eventually developed into laying hens, so I was assigned the task of obtaining customers for mother's productive birds. Any eggs that the family didn't consume and were not sold to customers, we took to the Dunnville Dairy for grading and sale through the dairy's store. One job that I also recall was having to paint the chicken roosts with used motor oil to kill resident hen lice.

Mother was an excellent cook and frequently prepared meals for our family or visitors. She had a habit of sometimes placing a can of peas in the oven to warm as she was preparing the rest of the main course. One afternoon, while I sat on the chesterfield in the peace and quiet of the living room, my brother Eldon was reading a newspaper beside me, and my father's attention was focused on his favourite television program. At the sound of an explosion from the kitchen, Eldon jumped to his feet. He skidded on the scatter rug as he tried to gain traction, on his way to the kitchen. I arrived at ground zero first, and found mother, her back to the wall, a dazed look on her face, as if to say, "Wot hoppened?"

Peas littered the kitchen floor, and the last pea from an exploded can was just rolling to a stop at my mother's feet. The oven door had blown backwards and hung limply by one hinge.

During the commotion, my father hadn't budged. When I returned to the living room and explained what happened, he simply looked over and muttered, "The damn fool." Being married for almost fifty years will perhaps temper your reaction to such an unexpected trauma that he'd probably seen coming long ago.

For her Eastern Star Lodge meetings, mother usually wore a stylish long white gown in which she felt that she looked very formal. On most days however, she wore her garden apparel consisting of a colourful floral kerchief wrapped around her head, floppy rubber boots, baggy bib overalls, and a threadbare wool sweater. This sartorial splendour was complemented by her pruning shears protruding from the back pocket of her overalls while a pair of work-gloves bulged out the pockets of her ratty wool sweater. On one occasion, I remember seeing mother in her gardening clothes, a hatchet in her right hand, while grasping one of her chickens by the neck as she manoeuvred the bird's neck over a chopping block. Once she had dispatched with the flopping fowl, her job then was to pluck and eviscerate the bird before it could be roasted, and finally its carcass boiled for chicken soup.

Like any kid, I had my share of pets, although mine might have been more unusual than those of most of my friends. My chief companion was Skipper, a tan coloured hound of questionable parentage. Skipper and I were inseparable until he was struck by a car and had to be put down by a vet. As a youngster attending Dunnville Public School, my weekends were usually occupied with fun. If I wasn't cycling around town, Skipper and I visited the bush at the farm on the end of John Street where I often wore a coonskin cap like the one worn by Davey Crockett. A bow and arrows added to my usual attire with a hunting knife in my belt just for good measure. Sources of amusement in the bush included building 'forts' and climbing trees. I would scale a mature tree then jump over to a nearby sapling. The sapling would gently lower me to the ground then spring back up once I let go. On occasion the sapling would break

and I'd land on my back with my wind knocked out. This didn't stop me however as I'd find another tree and repeat the manoeuvre.

In addition to Skipper, I owned a black Lab for a short time, assorted cats, tropical fish, the odd mud turtle and white rats. I received a white rat as a gift, but it turned out to be a female, and pregnant, thus producing several offspring. I enjoyed letting the rats run up my arm and perch on my shoulder, but my sister Ruby was not crazy about this performance.

An encounter with a skunk although not really a pet, did teach me a lesson. On a Saturday morning as I was heading downtown, I noticed a skunk ambling along the opposite side of the street. The animal weaved drunkenly, sometimes meandering onto the roadway. Its eyes were encrusted with mucus and it didn't seem to be able to see. In a

moment of stupidity, I slipped in behind the skunk, grabbed it by the base of the tail with my right hand, and the scruff of the neck with my left. The animal hissed and snapped as it tried to bite me. I was careful to keep the critter's lethal rear end pointed away from me, but while I was avoiding being bitten, I became too engrossed with the snapping front end, and forgot that skunks have two dangerous ends! My forgetfulness resulted in me getting sprayed in the face by the end that I'd been neglecting. I dropped the potential pet and headed home to a tongue lashing from mother, along with a good scrubbing with tomato juice then soap and water. The incident was a good learning experience in that it did expose me to the possible hazards of rabies in wild animals.

9 Dunnville High School Daze

Grade 8 Class

In 1952, I graduated from elementary to secondary school where during my five years at Dunnvile High School, the principal E. J. Hellyer was my chemistry teacher. I was particularly proficient in E. J.'s class. Off-and-on I would read above and beyond the curriculum when it came to the subject of chemistry. E. J. often asked me questions about chemistry topics that few others in the class were able to answer. In our agriculture-science class taught by Arthur Thompson, one of our activities was to sketch a variety of seeds. I often pocketed various samples and planted them in our garden when I got home. In one instance, I actually discovered from scoffed specimens that peanuts grew underground like potatoes. I particularly enjoyed mathematics taught by Claude Miller even though Claude often displayed two annoying habits. These included grasping a student by the ear lobe when he wanted to gain their attention, or snapping a student's knuckles with a ruler. Now that I think about it, during my own teaching years later, I adopted one of his habits. If students were noisy I would snap a yard stick on the front desk. This would often scare the hell of some unsuspecting young female student sitting near the front of the room. After nearly frightening her to death, I couldn't keep a straight face, thus spoiling the effect of my action which was intended to silence the boisterous class.

I didn't quite see eye-to-eye with my English teacher, Nelson Campbell in high school. One year I was exempt from writing the final exams due to high overall marks, so Nelson zapped me with a mark of 50% in English. I believe this was just because I avoided writing his final exam. It is ironic that in later life, when I took up writing, I fell back on one of my weakest subjects (English). Maybe old Nelson got the last laugh on me after all without me realizing it until now. I always enjoyed English Composition, but was not enamoured with English Literature. As I aged, I seemed to enjoy poetry and literature more. I would guess that as you mature, your attitude towards certain subjects matures as well. As an example of the incongruity of it all, long after I left high school, I agreed to write English essays for Marg Harper when she was studying a University of Toronto English course. I recall wring essays on Moby Dick and King Lear. Marg ended up getting 80% in the course. Oh, where is the logic in life if I could obtain barely 50% at times, but honours at the university level? There is no doubt in my mind that somewhere during my life I was bitten by a literary bug which over the years has caused me to spend untold hundreds of dollars on books. I'm sure that Nelson Campbell is still chuckling in his grave over how my literary bent has gotten my life completely bent out of shape. How could I being so lousy in English (even at Queen's University) and still be able to publish two books and a gaggle of columns for the Orangeville Banner newspaper?

While at Dunnville High School, I took Latin (instead of typing) and I have since studied German at university and Spanish at night school and in the evenings. I recently read a book which commented on the fact that mastering a new language was one way to help combat the onset of Alzheimer's. Isn't it strange how all of this ties together in life? Gertrude Rourke ('Gert') was my French instructor in high school. She stood about the height of a fire hydrant in stature, but was as tough as nails and an excellent language teacher. I believe that if necessary, I could function in French even today if I had to, thanks to Gert's efforts. The tag-team husband-and-wife duo of Douglas and Isabel Gordon taught Latin and history to me while I was at high school. The Latin phrase, "Cum copiis in Italia haemamomas" which translates as, "We were wintering with the troops in Italy" was frequently quoted to me by Russell Daley when I worked with him as a milk delivery boy in Dunnville. I'm sure that his Latin phrase is completely garbled after all these years, but a linguist could probably figure out what the correct phrase should be. To summarize languages in my life, I failed, but speak English. I am mildly fluent in French (due to Gert's influence) studied German for two years at university and Spanish at night school and during my retirement years in Orangeville. I have looked into Swahili and Icelandic to a very minor degree. Who knows? Will it take a study of Mandarin to combat the onset of losing some of my little gray cells completely due to Alzheimer's when I become as old as Methuselah?

I seem to be meandering away from my high school days, so must get back on track, but I guess really, all of my rambling is related?

My high school sporting life included gymnastics, in the form of tumbling. I recall at least one instance when I performed on stage at some school event. I did a headstand with my legs parted in a V as fellow students dove between my legs then continued into a forward roll. I was fortunate that there were no accidents which might have raised my voice an octave or two after a misdirected dive by one of my fellow gymnasts. I was too short to play basketball, and too tiny a twerp for football. I did try the latter, but gave it up in favour of soccer which stressed conditioning and trickiness which are more my style.

Since our chemistry teacher Elmo J. Hellyer was also the principal, he was often late at the start of our chemistry classes due to having to tend to his administrative duties. It is a bit much to expect that a collection of students left unsupervised for any length of time would not get into some form of devilment of their own devising. In our case we sat on lab stools facing a Bunsen-burner and bottles of sulphuric, nitric and hydrochloric acids within easy reach. A favourite pastime for some of us was to drop a copper penny into nitric acid in a beaker. The result of this chemical reaction was the production of a cloud of noxious brown fumes that billowed up from the beaker. Glass cupboards along the wall of the classroom contained a variety of other chemicals, magnesium being one of those forbidden ones with which we experimented. The fact that these cupboards were unlocked gave us a wider choice of chemicals with which to experiment. We were often cautioned, but no one was ever caught with their fingers in this chemical cookie jar, so to speak. When E. J. lumbered in through the classroom doorway, his nose would twitch like that of a groundhog sniffing the air. I suspect that from the fumes that E. J. inhaled he could tell exactly what we had been up to before he arrived.

There was only one occasion when I was ever called to appear before the principal. As it turned out, this was in error. During my high school career, I appeared from time-to-time in school plays. One day I entered a store room where we were practising for a performance. A teacher saw me leave that room during the day. It happened that girls' sanitary napkins began to show up in conspicuous places around the school. Since the napkins were stored in the room from which I was seen leaving, putting two and two together, it was assumed that I was the culprit responsible for this misdirected activity. When I explained the facts about my reason for being in the store room, the matter was dropped. I don't recall who was actually the guilty person, or if they were ever caught.

10 The Perfesser at Work

Grade 11 High School Phys. Ed. Class

I carried my interest in chemistry beyond the classroom. When father remodeled the kitchen in our John Street house, I took over a counter which he stored in the basement. The purchase of several various sized beakers, flasks, and glass tubing from a chemical supply store in Hamilton satisfied my interest in experimenting. It was probably at this stage that brother Wayne began to refer to me as 'Perfesser' rather than 'Twerp.'

While browsing through items at a garage sale one day, I discovered a copy of a book of formulae. The one item in the book which caught my eye was a formula for gunpowder. Since the required supplies of saltpetre, sulphur and charcoal were available at a local pharmacy I obtained enough of each to mix up a quantity of the powder and used it to manufacture my own high-powered firecrackers. Gathering a supply of used 12 gauge shotgun shells, with the dead firing cap removed, I inserted a firecracker wick rolled in cloth into the tiny hole in each. When I filled the spent casing with my gunpowder and taped the end, voila, I had powerful firecrackers.

My one mishap with the formula was not actually my fault. John Brunskill was a happy-go-lucky chum of mine who lived on Forest Street. John quit school to work and bought a Chrysler Saratoga luxury car. He spent much of his time picking up local chicks in town but since John and I were friends, I decided to share my gunpowder formula with him. One Saturday morning, I received a phone call from John saying that he wanted to demonstrate for me the gunpowder that he'd mixed up.

I jumped onto my bicycle and raced over to John's house, a two-story white frame one on Forest Street. The family had a barn out back and a garden shed attached to the side of their house. The shed with a cement floor contained just a wooden workbench, but little else. John produced a large apple juice can about a quarter full of his gunpowder mixture. Placing the partially filled can on the bench, he removed a small sample and dumped it onto a lid also nearby.

When John ignited the sample, it flared up and a few sparks settled into the tin containing the rest of his mixture. The contents didn't explode, but began to sputter and emit billowing clouds of smoke. The container turned cherry red from the heat as its contents blazed. In an attempt to contain the burning contents, I shoved a second juice can over the top hoping to smother the conflagration. When this didn't succeed, I used a stick to force the cherry-red container off the bench onto the floor. When the cans landed on the floor, there was a hell of a KAWUMP!!!

The room was filling with smoke, so we rushed outside for

fresh air. A container of yellow powdered sulphur had spilled on the floor as we scampered outside. We tracked sulphur which left a set of yellow footprints, marking the path of our exit across the grass. Looking back at the shed's doorway, clouds of smoke continued to belch out of the opening.

It was at this point that John's massive irate Scottish father limped with his cane out the back doorway and onto the porch. He bellowed, "What the fook is going on oot heere?" In no uncertain terms, he ordered me to leave and never darken their door again. There was no permanent damage to the house as a result of the accident, but my reputation was certainly left in tatters after the smoke had cleared.

As a form of apology, several days later, John showed up at my house with several sticks of dynamite. I believe that he had pilfered them from the storage shed of some construction site near town. Even though there were no blasting caps with the dynamite, I felt very uneasy storing the explosive sticks around the house and eventually buried them in mother's petunia bed to dispose of them. That was half a century ago. To the best of my knowledge, they are still buried at 703 John Street waiting to be discovered. Fortunately mother never unearthed the hidden cache while she was performing her gardening chores. If she had discovered them, that might have given new meaning to the expression, 'bursting out into bloom.' My experiments with explosives did not end with the John Brunskill experience, however.

While reading a copy of the Toronto Star Weekly, I came across an article about an amateur rocket society in California. The fuel used to power the rockets was a mixture of zinc dust and sulphur. I was familiar with the sulphur but knew nothing about zinc dust. From a casual conversation with my father, I learned that zinc dust was used in the processing of gold at the McIntyre Mine in Schumacher where father used to work. A letter to the mine, disclosed their supplier's address in the USA, and I was able to order 10 pounds of dust. As a result of my efforts, a gallon can of zinc dust arrived from California. It didn't take long for me to discover a suitable mix of the two components to produce my brand of rocket fuel. One noticeable product of the ignited mixture was more white smoke than was produced by my gunpowder. I soon produced more firecrackers powered by my rocket fuel rather than the less powerful gunpowder.

This led to the production of my version of a bazooka. My new weapon consisted of a cast iron fence post one end of which I sealed off with a wooden plug. Since mother at that time was in the act of disposing of a ringer washing machine, I commandeered one of its hard rubber ringers, and taped it to fit snuggly into the cast iron pipe. If I lit one of my zinc bombs and tossed it down the tube, then slid the taped rubber ringer in after it, the weapon was armed. Holding the apparatus on my shoulder like a bazooka, the explosion propelled the projectile 100 feet or more. I carried out my test firings in a sandpit where I could view the trajectory of the fired roller. In hindsight, I was obviously unaware of the possibility of metal fatigue. The cast iron pipe could have exploded if the metal became weakened, and might have taken my head off. (Oh the foolishness of youth!!)

Looking back from 2014 at my manufacture of explosives in the 1950's, I realize how much times have changed. Although I was careful handling my explosives as a kid, if I performed the same experiments with gunpowder today, I would likely be considered to be a terrorist, or at the very least, be locked up as a juvenile delinquent. It is with some sense of irony that I notice that my experiments with explosives appears in this memoir just before my relationship with a supreme court judge. I'm sure David Marshall would have made an interesting comment if I had described this incident to him.

I usually reserved my use of rocket fuel to manufacture a relatively harmless supply of firecrackers. I lit them and, like a grenade, tossed them into the distance where they exploded with a burst of dense white smoke causing no real damage.

I had many friends in high school, but one of my closest was David Marshall whose father was a doctor in Dunnville. David and I were usually in the same grades during most of our years in school. Since we both had red hair and freckles, we were often confused with one another. It was during his last two years at DHS that David left to attend the private school Ridley College. I lost touch with most of my school chums but did contact David again after a hiatus of approximately half a century. Since his chosen career was so unique, as was David, I've included my following story of David as it appeared in my *Meandering Through Life* column in the February 11, 2010 edition of the *Orangeville Banner Newspaper*.

11 Doctor, Lawyer, Indian Chief, Supreme Court Judge

Mr. Justice Thomas David
Colbeck Haydon Marshall
1939 - 2009

"There's my man!" were the first words of greeting from a friend I had not seen for half a century. I had been lounging in an easy chair in the law library of the Cayuga Provincial Court House. My panoramic view was one of shelves, extending from floor to ceiling, bursting with dusty leather bound law books. The Honourable Justice David Marshall, wearing his black official judge's robes, arrived to greet me. His beaming smile and hearty handshake left little doubt that David was pleased that I had made the effort 'to nourish our friendship lifelong' as he later inscribed in a complimentary copy of Dr. Marshall's *History of Haldimand County*.

In the early 1950s, David Marshall and I were freckle

faced, red-haired lads of the same age who could have been mistaken for twins. We hung out together and cooperated regularly on homework assignments.

To quote New York Yankees baseball catcher Yogi Berra, "If you come to a fork in the road, take it!" Following our high school years, our lives followed distinctly different paths. I chose to devote thirty-four years to pursue a career as a teacher of high school mathematics. David first became a medical doctor, then a lawyer, and was later appointed to the position of Justice of the Supreme Court of the Northwest Territories and Yukon. Having obtained his pilot's licence, Justice Marshall fulfilled his obligations as a judge by providing a rolling court as he flew his aircraft through the north, resolving native Innuit cases. To provide more reasoned verdicts when dealing with these judgements, he learned the Inuktatuk language. David's last appointment was to the highest honorary position in the Armed Forces, as Colonel Commandant, serving as liaison between the military and the Royal Family.

Mr. Justice Thomas David Colbeck Haydon Marshall received many citations and much recognition for his exemplary medical and legal accomplishments but never at the expense of his humanitarian side. An excerpt from David's 2009 journal best exemplifies his attitude. "Kindness to all, always. Hard work will lead to success but kindness to all is most important."

Considering all his titles and accomplishments, those who never met David might expect him to be an officious stuffed shirt. On the contrary. Of all the titles David had, the one he valued most was to say he was your friend. David has been described as, "intelligent, accomplished, fair, principled, respected, and loved by all." He would talk with anyone, anytime, anywhere. You could meet 'Doc' at Tim Hortons, on a sidewalk or at a yard sale. He was part of the community and always had time to speak to anyone.

While stationed in the Northwest territories and East Arctic, David treated patients at a government hospital and provided regular onsite care to remote native communities. Later in his career, he served as a medical missionary, treating natives in Ecuador. But it was for his work with the Six Nations Indian Reserve near Cayuga that he received the title of honorary Iroquois Chief. In addition to the accomplishments already mentioned, David found time to create oil paintings, author seven texts, lecture at several universities, work on behalf of the mentally handicapped, dabble in politics, raise cattle, ride horses, collect old books, and incongruously squeeze in time to study diesel mechanics.

After my meeting with David on December 13, 2007 in Cayuga, we remained in contact and planned a follow up meeting in Cambridge, a convenient location midway between Cayuga and Orangeville. Waiting to settle on another meeting date, my procrastination taught me a cruel lesson. I received word in November 2009 that David had died suddenly from complications following surgery.

David's funeral service on Friday November 27, 2009, at St. Paul's Anglican Church in Dunnville was a full military one. This included a Scottish piper, colour party, flag-draped coffin and all of the pomp and circumstance that he richly deserved. The overflow crowds of mourners at both the visitation and funeral service were indicative of the affection in which David was held. For the journey to his final resting place at Riverside Cemetery on the shore of the Grand River, David's coffin was transported in a polished black horse-drawn hearse preceded by two dapple gray Belgians. A trailing rider-less mount with empty riding boot in the right stirrup represented the void left in the world by the loss of a truly amazing man and good friend.

Addendum: In December 2007, as David and I sat chatting

in a Chinese restaurant on the main street of Cayuga, we shared a lunch of chicken fried rice, egg foo yong and a variety of other oriental delicacies. He shared the following story with me which inspired the following cartoon:

In David's words: "I'd served my time in the North and stopped at Edmonton on my way to Southern Ontario. When time for lunch arrived, I left my hotel and from the sidewalk hailed a passing taxi. Slipping into the back seat, I gave the cab driver the name of my favourite restaurant. As I settled back, I had a chance to get a closer look at the driver, and realized that he was a man that I had recently sentenced to a prison term on an assault charge. Not wishing to create an incident, I tapped him on the shoulder. 'excuse me, could you stop at the next corner, I just remembered something that I forgot to do. It's only a short walk back to my hotel.' The driver perhaps never recognized who I was, but later I could enjoy a meal thinking, 'It's better to be safe than sorry.'"

I sent the cartoon original to David and have since with reference to newspaper photos reworked the drawing to improve

David's caricature but the gist of the cartoon has otherwise remained the same.

In an August 2012 FLASHBACK in the Hamilton Spectator newspaper in '*This Day In History*' an article about David Marshall reminded me of two facts not mentioned in my original story. First, he became executive director of the National Judicial Institute, the country's first school for judges in 1988. Second, he made headlines in 2006 when he issued an injunction ordering native protestors to leave the Douglas Creek Estates housing project in Caledonia, but they refused. His order was later overturned by a higher court. Even following his death in 2009, it appears as though David's impact on our society has not been forgotten.

Clare's bedroom in Dunnville

12 Tote that Barge, Lift that Bale

Looking back at my activities during my teenage years, I am surprised at how much I was able to cram into that time! It is my feeling that this may have been due to the work ethic which I inherited from my parents. One could certainly not say that I was lazy. As I have already mentioned, my earliest jobs included working in the family garden and peddling vegetables and eggs around Dunnville for my mother. I had a paper route as well and did some pin setting at Dunnville's bowling alley. During the summer, I picked tomatoes at farms in the area. These along with cucumbers and beans, were purchased by Canadian Canners on the edge of town. I believe this company, besides canning tomatoes and juice, also produced ketchup and Bick's pickles. It was likely late in my public school career that I worked at the Grand Theatre movie house in Dunnville, a long thin building with a central aisle and rows of seats on either side. My job was to clean up popcorn, gum wrappers and other garbage after shows and there were times when I also had to scrape gum from the bottom of seats.

In addition to my cleaning duties, I distributed advertising posters to establishments in town. As shows changed, I had to continually update displays around town and in the front of the theatre. I can't recall if I received cash for my duties, but one thing that I did receive was unlimited freedom to attend as many shows as I wished. This was the era of the serial, so I could follow episodes of Superman, Rocket Man, Lash Laru, Zorro, The Lone Ranger, Tom Mix, and whatever other heroes were in vogue at the time. I enjoyed such entertainers as the Three Stooges, Laurel and Hardy, Abbott and Costello, Humphrey Bogart, Roy Rogers, Gene

Autry, and extravaganzas and specials such as *Gone WithThe Wind*, and *The Kon-Tiki Expedition*, as they were featured.

If this memoir is to include consideration of lifelong learning, I would have to say that my exposure to these films, which included cartoons, was an opportunity for my imagination to be massaged frequently. I would put my job at the Grand in the same league as listening to the radio when it comes to having encouraged the development of my imagination.

Looking back at my job working for the Grand Theatre, it was the first time I ever heard my prim and proper mother swear! While I watched my movie heroes, one which caught my eye was Zorro. This swashbuckler wore a slim black mask over his eyes, and with his rapier carved a Z on villains. Since I had no mask, I snooped around our house until I discovered a black velvet dress that my mother had stashed away in our attic. Assuming (incorrectly) that this piece of material belonged in the rag bag, I cut out a large enough hunk to create my own Zorro mask. When mother discovered what I had done to her velvet dress, it was the first time that I ever heard her explode and use the word damn. (I think that the expletive actually contained the phrase "damn fool.")

While I am on the topic of swashbucklers and masks, a second instance comes to mind. It was more related to knights, perhaps in the King Arthur era. I fancied making a helmet of the type worn in battles. For the project I started with a cylindrical, used, one-gallon Quaker State motor oil can. With tin snips, I sliced out the bottom to expose my mouth, and left a strip to protect my nose, then cut out eye holes. When I slipped the mask over my head to try it for size, my first thought was, "I wonder if I can get this thing off?" Imagine my embarrassment if I couldn't get the mask off and had to wear it to school the next week. Shades of *The Man in the Iron Mask*! but it did come off okay.

As my age increased, so too did opportunities for higher

paying jobs. The first was work at the Dunnville Dairy, producers of Puritan Quality Dairy Products. James N. Allen who was once our Provincial Minister of Highways owned the dairy but his son Harvey took over the operation of the business while I worked there. It was at this time that Puritan products were delivered by horse and wagon, the milkman being Malcolm Bowden who also served as the town's fire chief. I never worked directly with the chief on his milk delivery route, but my brother Eldon did.

Some of the tasks I performed at the dairy included working in the ice house where 300 pound blocks of ice were produced then reduced to smaller blocks for sale to the public. I also worked with Art Daymon, the butter maker. Art operated a large circular wooden butter churn. One of my jobs was to plunk great gobs of butter into the hopper of a machine that formed and wrapped pounds of the finished product. It amused me that the butter wrappers advertised, "Untouched by human hands." What was I, with butter up to my elbows as I packed it into a hopper from which an auger pressed it into the finished pound?

Since Art was also the cheese man, I recall having to turn round wooden containers of aging cheddar cheese in a storage room where cheddar was kept until it was sufficiently ripe. Puritan cheddar cheese was a product highly sought by US visitors who motored across Lake Erie by yacht each year. Packaging ice cream was another of my duties. I would often report for work in the middle of the summer wearing a parka since I worked in the freezer at times loading trucks with ice cream products. Anyone who saw me on my way to work probably thought I was out of my mind dressed that way in the middle of summer. For at least two years during my high school career, a chum Howard Roth and I operated a service for the dairy whereby from our insulated truck we sold cream, eggs, ice and other dairy products to cottagers along the shore of Lake Erie.

Holy Cow!!

During my high school career while I was still working at the Dunnville Dairy during the summer, I accepted a position working for Russell Samuel Daley, the owner-operator of Jerseydale Farm Dairy. Russ would show up in town daily in his G.M. sedan delivery or pickup, usually in the evening around 5 o'clock. My job was to assist him as a milk delivery boy during the week and each evening until approximately 9 o'clock. It was obviously a job that was suitable for the evenings after school had finished for the day.

Russ operated his business from his farm at Rainham Centre, approximately five miles along the Rainham Road, not far from Lake Erie. Russell was a cheery, rosy cheeked man in his sixty's with the weathered complexion of a farmer, a slightly bulbous nose and shock of dishevelled gray hair. When Russ was a kid, he promised his dying father that he would look after his mother as long as she lived. As a result of this promise, Russ remained single until the age of seventy. While I worked with Russ, he treated me like the son that he never had. He owned and rented out several apartments in Dunnville, and even found time to build the odd house in town. Russ urged me to continue my education and served as an excellent role model.

Completing homework was never a problem while I worked with Russ. Often I would complete assignments while he gabbed with some of his customers. For Russ, chatting with town's folk was probably one of the most enjoyable aspects of his business. During the time I spent working with Russ, he sold milk in glass bottles. Products included regular milk with cream settling to the top, but he also sold skim, cream, and chocolate milk. During the winter, it was not unusual to see frozen milk push the caps upward, making the bottles resemble a row of miniature soldiers standing in line. Russ often jokingly referred to his business as Jerseydale Skim Milk Dairy. Customers frequently left notes and change in bottles for orders to be filled, or milk received. Russ related one instance when he traditionally placed the milk directly into the refrigerator for a customer. One day when he rapped on the door and popped into the kitchen, bottles in hand, he encountered a visiting couple, naked and passionately embracing one another up against a kitchen wall. Red-faced Russ left the order on the table, and retreated as discreetly as possible.

During his early years in business in the 1940s, Russ delivered milk to an airport between Dunnville and Port Maitland on Lake Erie at the mouth of the Grand River. This airfield was a training base for RCAF pilots flying Harvard aircraft during the Second World War. Russ used to entertain me with stories of happenings at the base. One amusing situation was based on Russell's manner of dress. He wore a peaked cap, and Sam Brown belt over one shoulder. His Sam Brown belt helped to keep the change device on the belt around his waist from pulling his pants down. His work clothes, belts, and peaked hat made it easy to confuse Russ with officers wandering about the base. New young trainees often mistook Russ for an officer and they would salute him without realizing their error. Not wishing to embarrass the novice airmen, Russ would return a snappy salute of his own.

While I worked with Russ and he was single, we considered 'the old maids and widders' as he referred to them, on the route as customers requiring his personal attention.

Russell once raised the champion Jersey of Canada. He eventually sold this Jersey cow, Sadie of Hillcrest, to a millionaire cattle breeder in Quebec. I believe this sale was the impetus and provided the financing for Russ to begin his own dairy business. It was not until I left high school for university that I quit working for Jerseydale Dairy, but we did keep in touch later after both he and I were married. I cherish memories of working with Russ, and will forever remember his favourite saying, "Just between me you and the gatepost." I guess during those years, he treated me as the gatepost, but I'd prefer the use of the term "confidant."

13 When the Rubber Hit the Road

The first automobile I purchased was a 1929 Model A Ford sedan. The Model A's previous owner Newt Lymburner had exceeded his 'best before date' when it came to driving. No longer able to qualify for a driving licence, Newt offered to sell his chariot to me for the princely sum of $45. I had to supply the vehicle with a new battery, and its tires were nearly bald, but in spite of those shortcomings, for me it was proudly my own first car.

An early problem I experienced with my purchase was that I didn't own a driver's license or for that matter did I even know how to drive! To overcome those hurdles, once I'd completed the transaction, my brother Gerry volunteered to drive my new Model A to our house and park it in our driveway. My next objective was then obviously to master the intricacies of the Model A so that I could drive it wherever I wanted to go. Russell Daley offered to give me driving lessons and get me on the road as soon as possible. He arrived in town one evening, took a stroll around my purchase, as he assessed what I'd gotten myself into. He placed his right foot on the running board, settled his right elbow onto his knee, and cupped his chin into his palm.

"Well, the sooner we start, the quicker you'll get to master the old girl." He made himself comfortable in the passenger seat as I clamoured into position behind the steering wheel. Russ placed his hand on the knob of the floor-mounted gear shift, and asked me to rest my right hand on top of his. While I depressed the clutch, he shifted several times through the gears so that I could get the feel of where each was located. He then explained that I had to press in the clutch, shift into first gear, then release the clutch and slowly increase pressure on the gas pedal.   After several jackrabbit attempts, I made it onto the roadway and following a few gear changes through the various forward speeds, I circled our block several times practicing that part of the lesson. Once in the driveway again, I experimented with reversing, then finished for the day. For the next few weeks he allotted enough time to give me a series of longer lessons and brother Gerry took me out several times until I was eventually able to apply for my license. The driving test was minimal, just another boring outing for the inspector. He eventually seemed satisfied with my progress after the very brief but casual test and granted me my licence.

Once I was able to drive solo, I discovered several faults of the vehicle that had not initially been obvious. As I slowed down, the well-worn front end would begin to shimmy. Since the brakes were mechanical and controlled by brake rods, it was difficult to keep them adjusted properly, consequently it was impossible for the brakes to provide a consistently reliable stop. Pushing the brake pedal to the floorboards, my purchase would come to a slow, but not always predictable halt. This resulted in me requiring an almost infinitely long stopping distance. I often thought if I had several cement blocks tied to a rope, and tossed them overboard, I'd have a more effective stopping mechanism. All in all, the faults of the Model A's brakes and the shimmy caused me to be more cautious during my motoring (mostly about town). On one outing, when I had to make a panic stop, I was forced to pull onto a grassy boulevard, round a hydro pole, and head back onto the pavement before I could bring the vehicle to a complete stop. The fact that this manoeuvre took place in front of the house of the chief of police just showed what a charmed life I led. Thankfully for me, the chief must have been out dealing with more serious lawbreakers further afield on that occasion.

I also learned that while I sat in the driveway with the car idling, if I revved up the engine and turned off the key, gas accumulating in the carburetor would ignite when I turned the key back on, and the car would backfire. This did not endear me to my mother, or any of my neighbours, but more importantly, it was hard on the engine. From time-to-time, if necessary, due to a weak battery, I could get the car started by using the hand crank. This could be a tricky procedure since a kick back while cranking might result in a broken thumb if the handle was not gripped properly. Without a crank handy for starting, in desperate cases, if the vehicle was pushed then the clutch released with the car in gear, the engine could be coaxed to start. Since gravity fed the fuel from the tank located just in front of the windshield, it has been said that the only tools necessary to repair a Model A Ford are a chunk of wire and a pair of pliers. If the gas line became clogged, pliers would loosen the line and the wire could then unblock the tubing. Since a 4-cylinder Model A was such a simple vehicle, it provided an excellent opportunity for a budding mechanic to learn how to repair an engine, adjust brakes, or perform countless other repairs that became essential just to keep my contraption roadworthy.

As was the case with most of Henry Ford's creations, mine was as black as a hearse. I rectified this situation with a brush and can of bilious sea foam green enamel thus transforming my vehicle immediately into a two-toned model. While I owned the 'old girl' most of my traveling was around Dunnville with the exception of making a few five mile excursions with friends to our swimming spot off the lighthouse pier at Port Maitland. The Model A provided me a couple of years of service until my brother-in-law Bob Plant took it off of my hands when he was in need of transportation himself.

Before I leave the subject of Model A's, It is worth relating a brief episode in the life of brother Eldon's Model A roadster. The convertible two-seated vehicle had a rumble seat which was put to use during a visit by cousin Denzil Roberts from South Africa. Eldon offered to take our cousin on a trip in his roadster to view Niagara Falls. During the return part of the trip in pouring rain, the roadster's engine died, resulting in a hasty visit to a garage for repairs which returned the vehicle to life. By the time my sister Ruby riding with me in the rumble seat finally arrived back in Dunnville, we ended up resembling drowned rats having just escaped from a sunken ship, while Eldon and cousin Denzil riding upfront remained relatively unsaturated during our ordeal in the rumble seat.

Once I had parted company with my Model A, what better place to buy a replacement than at Pearson's Scrap Yard on the edge of Dunnville. I purchased my next vehicle for $75, a 1932 McLaughlin Buick coupe. This elevated me into elegance in the automobile world. My new set of wheels resembled a machine which might have been owned by mobster Al Capone. Its features included two immense chrome headlights, a spare tire mounted on each front fender, a fixed canvas top, scroll work on each side of the roof, a blind on the rear window, a rumble seat in back and adjustable vertical grills out front. The beauty was a dark forest green colour, with whitewalls, and mechanical cable brakes. A grease fitting, just beneath each door allowed the owner to grease many points connected by copper tubing. A straight 8-cylinder engine that looked large enough to power a Mac truck or perhaps even The Queen Elizabeth ocean liner loomed under the long low hood.

The Buick's body work, its fenders the thickness of a boiler plate, would have put a WWII armoured car to shame. Much of the body was solid hardwood and I'm sure that if my Buick had collided with a modern day car, it would carve open today's models as if a can opener had been used. One drawback of the car's excessive weight was the fact that the rear springs were inadequate (to put it mildly). Whenever I hit a bump, the Buick floundered like a hippopotamus trying to balance on a surfboard. An opportunity to correct the sluggish rear springs occurred when my Buick's driveshaft broke. At a wrecking yard, I bought a replacement from a 1932 Buick sedan. Since the sedan had springs heavier than those of the coupe, I simply replaced my Buick's complete driveshaft and rear end and spring assembly with that of the much heavier vehicle.

I eventually sold the McLaughlin back to Pearson's Scrap yard for $75. Sadly for me, that Buick would be worth thousands of dollars today once it was restored. The lad who next purchased my Buick from the wrecking yard had the intention of restoring the car but may never have realized that the rear end assembly was not original equipment. But who knows, maybe he discovered the fault eventually. If not, there is an impostor Buick with a beefed-up rear end out there somewhere in the world.

Following my sale of the Buick, I purchased a 1935 Ford V8 coupe on which the previous owner had installed motorcycle fenders up front, in place of the original ones. The contraption showed the wear-and-tear of a relic that escaped from a stock car racing track, so it wasn't long before I replaced the V8, filling the void with an early 50's red Morris Minor convertible.

For reasons I still find inexplicable, the early history of my purchasing the Morris Minor is shrouded in a dense fog. I do know that I bought the convertible from a used-car lot in Hamilton. I believe the price was $140, but even that figure could be challenged. I was still a high school student at the time and likely succumbed to the smooth talking of a slick car salesman. The seller arranged for the Minor to be delivered to my home in Dunnville after I had agreed to the deal. Why I made this delivery arrangement, I'm still not entirely sure. Perhaps the salesman wasn't convinced that my chariot would be able to make the trip to

Dunnvile (all of 35 miles) under its own power. My memories of the Morris Minor are composed of experiences from the instant the salesman drove the little convertible into our driveway. Why is it I always discover shortcomings of vehicles I've purchased, after all cash involved has left my hands? Perhaps it may be some distorted version of the learning experience as it applies to me! Overriding factors for my purchase of the Morris Minor were two. First it was a convertible, and second, it was red. What I eventually discovered was floor boards with as many holes as a Swiss cheese. Talk about viewing my purchase through rose-coloured glasses! I couldn't see the forest for the trees, or in this case the holes for the rust. The convertible top had no holes in it, but it definitely had leaked, causing the floor to rust through in countless places. Looking at it from a positive point of view, with the number of rusted-out holes in the floor, there was no fear of any further water pooling, on the floor once it leaked in.

The tiny four-cylinder engine hiding under the bonnet could just barely muster the breakneck speed of a good brisk walk but I must admit it usually got me from A to B, although not with the speed that I had hoped for. I was probably in my final year of high school when I made the purchase. This gave me time during the summer to test drive my new set of wheels before I even dreamed of driving it to Kingston from Dunnville. On a sunny summer afternoon, I was motoring east of Dunnville when I felt a bump and the rear left corner of the car dropped down. Glancing to my left, I watched my rear wheel roll by. The rolling rubber followed the centre white line of the road, missed oncoming traffic, and veered left into a roadside ditch. My rear driver's-side wheel hub had dropped to the pavement, the loose wheel enroute down the road, splitting the rear fender, and slightly flattening the brake drum. When I stopped and caught up to the wheel in the ditch, I discovered a wheel nut inside the wheel's hubcap which had remained attached. Apparently I'd lost a cotter pin from the end of the axel, allowing the wheel nut to spin off. That was when all Hell broke loose! After recovering the lost wheel, I jacked up the left rear axle, hammered out the brake drum, remounted the lost wheel, replaced the wheel nut using a new cotter pin, and was soon on the road home again.

Following my car repairs, I eventually dismantled my lab in the basement and quit the production of explosives before heading off to university. My high school math teacher, Claude Miller was my inspiration to attend Queen's University in Kingston when I graduated from high school in 1957. An attraction at Queen's was Claude's math instructor, a professor Red Miller, but I never did have Red as a professor while I was at Queen's.

After I had completed my Queen's registration, I packed my belongings, took a bus to Hamilton, then to Toronto and finally a train to Kingston. Queen's student residence McNeil House became my home for my first year at university. This gave me the opportunity to become acclimatized to university life in Kingston for the first year. Since my roommate. Bill Edwards, who had failed his previous year was repeating it again and he came from nearby Napanee, I got to meet Bill's friends Don Creighton, Harley Osborne, and Dave Phippen who were all from Napanee as well.

I shall attempt to summarize my four years at Queen's by recounting a number of academic facts along with at least as many nonacademic ones. Hopefully these will paint a picture of a completely different life in Kingston that was not all work and no play. I enrolled in a General Arts Degree for the first year with courses that I selected aiming me towards an Honours degree in Physics, but once I discovered that I preferred Mathematics to Physics (and that Physics was a very tough subject) I decided to switch to a 4-year Specialist's degree in Mathematics with the objective of becoming a High School mathematics teacher. I just stumbled into the teaching option, mainly because all of my Napanee cronies were making that choice as well. My course selections began to broaden out once I had decided upon my future occupation. This allowed me to study Philosophy, Psychology, Geography, English, and conversational German. I had several Physics courses under my belt, tried but dropped Astronomy, and in the end focused on math. During this time, I felt my way along, taking courses more for interest but ones that would complement my mathematics degree.

Queen's Frosh

        Quite often I accompanied the Napanee boys to downtown Kingston restaurants where we gathered for supper. Dave Phippen and I would frequently start a chess game in his room and carry the same game on for days until there was finally a winner. During my first year at McNeil House, I came home for Christmas, and while in Dunnville, I contracted chicken pox from my nephew Rick. When I returned to the student residence, the medics sent me for a two week stint in the isolation ward of Kingston Hospital until I got over the contagious stage and could return without infecting others. My companion in crime in isolation, Charlie Burbank, whom I'd never met previously was an engineer. We whiled away some of our time playing checkers, using aspirin that we should have been consuming to combat the chicken pox.

Since I still owned my Morris Minor convertible, I used it to commute between Dunnville and Kingston on occasion. My set of wheels had trouble keeping up with other traffic on the highways (and particularly up hills). The winter was usually tough sledding, partly due to an inadequate heater. A set of red-flannel long-johns would have been a welcome addition to my driving gear during the frosty winter season. In addition to a lousy heater, rusted-out holes in the flooring caused my posterior to freeze during the frigid part of the year. The rusty gaps in the floor acted like air scoops as they gobbled up great gusts of freezing air along my route. Besides frigid air, snow also got sucked into my rust bucket, but in spite of these hazards, I did manage to survive the season without suffering from hypothermia or a bad case of frostbite.

Since I was always thinking about summer employment to earn a bit of cash for the following school year, I decided to join the URTP (University Reserve Training Program). This would have meant I would become affiliated with the RCAF and could choose to become a Flying Control Officer working in the control tower of an airbase once I graduated from Queen's. The only actually compulsory part of the training was that I had to serve 4 summers working for the air force. At Queen's, we had weekly lectures in the evening on a variety of general interest topics such as finances and politics. I spent my first summer as a cadet in training at College Militaire

Royal De St. Jean in St. Jean Quebec. My cadet training continued with a course at Camp Borden, and in the summer of year two I spent my time at Downsview airport in Toronto in the control tower. I had to serve the final stint after I graduated from university because I'd begun the program in my second year. As a student at Queen's, I did not consider myself to be a gifted academic. My success was due to effort and hard work rather than a result of superior brain power. I rewrote a couple of courses (English and History) thus managing to squeeze out enough credits to qualify for a 4-year degree with a specialist in mathematics. I did not earn a lot of money during the summers affiliated with the RCAF, but it guaranteed summer jobs including room and board and it was a more unusual learning opportunity than I might have experienced otherwise.

The final fourth year summer obligations with my cadet training found me assigned to Trenton airfield. Since that base was responsible for manning Resolute Bay in Canada's Northwest Territories, I agreed to spend my last two months satisfying my government obligations by hanging out with the Innuit, polar bears and seals in that land of the midnight sun. A lumbering twin-engine turboprop RCAF C-119 Flying boxcar provided my transportation. I left Trenton in June of 1961, and was flying via Winnipeg when a blizzard at Resolute forced us to land in Churchill, Manitoba until the storm abated. I attempted to catch flights further north, but on each occasion was 'bumped' by Innuits with higher priority than I had. I believe I spent a week meandering around Churchill visiting such highlights as a native museum staffed by a Roman Catholic priest, and a shop with the colourful name 'Torchie's el Centro.' I finally did catch a flight out, but Mother Nature once again altered my destination, sending the craft to land at the American air base in Thule, Greenland. The Americans provided digs and meals until we were able to carry on to Resolute the next day.

14 Intoxicating Prose

The moonscape of Resolute Bay consisted of a packed gravel runway and living quarters of plywood-connected tunnels joining sleeping accommodations, mess hall and lounge area. Because air traffic was minimal, I did manage to get aloft once in the cockpit of an aircraft to view the surroundings. There wasn't a tree in sight, just a few scrawny bushes and the odd sprout of growth. My closest encounter to a polar bear was to view its hide hanging on a clothesline in Resolute. Two prospectors camping out on the ice were sleeping in a small tent. One fellow awoke and found himself facing a polar bear. He reached for his rifle, but the bear grabbed him by the arm and dragged the man out of his sleeping bag. The second prospector woke up and shot the bear, thus the bear's head headed to a lab where it was tested for rabies, and its hide ended up hanging on an Innuit clothesline to cure.

My recreation at Resolute (drinking beer) involved a male RCMP constable assigned to the base. He introduced me to the drinking game 'St. Peter, & St. Paul.' Sitting more or less in a circle, participants each received names, St. Peter, St. Paul, #1, #2, #3, etc., depending on the number of participants. St. Peter would start off singing, "St. Peter to one of the members of the group, perhaps #6". Without missing a beat, #6 would carry the tune, "#6 to another member." As the singing continued, anyone who missed a beat would have to take a slug of booze. Participants had to pay attention whenever their number was called. If you missed your number and the rhythm, and had to take a drink, you could soon become polluted. Naturally, those numbers most frequently called were soon under the table, and when drinkers became too intoxicated or bored, the game eventually ended. Since I was never much of a drinker, this game did little to further my search for knowledge. Thus ended this segment of my university education, as I headed back down south to civilization (?) as a fully qualified Flying Officer in The Royal Canadian Air Force.

Before I put to bed the exposure of my university days, I'd like to admit to two final university experiences which might be revealing. The door to all jobs, aside from teaching, was not completely shut while I was at Queen's. To test the waters in a different field, I appeared for an interview as an International Trade Commissioner with the Canadian Government. (This may have been on a bit of a whim and perhaps wasn't completely thought out beforehand.) I attributed my failure to be accepted for the job as being due to my lack of sufficient background courses such as History and Politics. Perhaps the Canadian government's loss is my gain?

My second drinking experience besides beer drinking in Resolute Bay concerns my third year at Queen's when I served my time in a private boarding house operated by an elderly landlady. While I was away from Dunnville, I did communicate with mother on a regular basis, and she reciprocated with newsy letters from the home front as well. During year three, I decided to write a letter home, and to help the process along, I purchased a mickey of Captain Morgan's rum and a large bottle of coke. I began by mixing a drink for myself, "Dear Mom," then swigged back a shot of rum with coke, and continued

to write. As one might expect, as I progressed with the drinks and letter writing, my script became more fluid and unintelligible. By the time I had completed the letter, and most of the tot of rum, my letter home looked like something composed by a lunatic. It was not a piece of creative correspondence that I would even consider sending to my prim and proper mother, thus the document ended up in the waste basket rather than the Royal Mails. I must have been completely nuts to have ever conceived of such a performance. Who knows, perhaps Ernest Hemingway might have been impressed with my soused letter writing effort, thinking I was attempting to create my version of *War and Peace.*

Ironically, the day after I completed writing in this memoir about my rum-soaked letter home, I noted an item in the New York Times Book Review in the Toronto Star Newspaper. The volume being reviewed, was titled, The *Trip To Echo Spring* by Olivia Laing. Olivia examined the "alcoholic insanity of six famous writers, namely John Cheever, Tennessee Williams, John Berryman, Ernest Hemingway, F. Scott Fitzgerald and Raymond Carver." The reviewer began the article with a quotation by Ernest Hemingway, "Modern life is often a mechanical oppression and liquor is the only mechanical relief." After reading the review, I immediately rushed to BookLore and ordered a copy of the book for my library. Exposure to this article jarred my sober little gray cells to ask, "How have experiences with the grapes of wrath affected my life and consequently the writing of this memoir and was Hemingway's quote an explanation for my alcoholic letter to mom?"

Examining the influence of alcohol during my life, the first incident that comes to mind following those already mentioned, took place in Brampton.

First a bit of background. It was not long after I began my teaching career, while my wife Dorothy worked in the lab of Peel

Memorial Hospital. Pat Robinson, a friend of Dorothy was a nurse, and she and her husband Terry invited us to visit their cottage in Muskoka for a weekend. The Robinsons were both British and Terry was a man whose height was well in excess of six feet. Terry spent time in the British army as a motorcycle courier, and laughed about times he and his buddies would visit British pubs during the war. If any disturbances ever erupted in their drinking establishments, the group would call on Terry to keep the peace. Terry would simply appear and 'loom' over any troublemakers. Terry's appearance usually settled any disturbance before it really began. What Terry's adversaries didn't realize was that he was actually a meek and mild man who was as gentle as a kitten, but for Terry, his 'looming' was always enough to settle any potential dispute.

Getting back to the Robinsons' cottage; one evening Terry's neighbour invited Terry and me over to view plans for an addition the neighbour was planning to add to his cottage. Being a considerate host, the neighbour offered us drinks which consisted of a shot of Canadian Club Whisky chased with a bottle of beer. These 'boilermakers' can be devastating, particularly to someone like me who was unaccustomed to such heavy-duty drinking. After several 'boilermakers' each (who was keeping count?) Terry and I were in sad shape by the time we decided to retreat back to the Robinsons' cottage for the night. My intoxicated condition was demonstrated by the fact that just before I got ready for bed, I inadvertently leaned on a red-hot space heater with my bare hand, and didn't even flinch. The next morning Dorothy asked, "Didn't you get burned last night when you leaned on the stove?" I replied, "No, are you disappointed?" It did create an incident that remains burned into my memory to this day. Was the fact that my hand was not scorched an example of 'mind over matter?' or was it 'booze over gray matter?'

My next memorable alcohol saturated outing could be blamed on my Irish heritage. While I was teaching in Orangeville (probably in the 1970s) I convinced two of my teaching colleagues to accompany me out to celebrate St. Patrick's Day (a Friday) at the Busholm Inn in Erin. This watering-hole seemed to be a logical place to celebrate an event intended to honour an Irish patron saint. We piled into one of the group's cars, a compact red Dodge Colt and blasted off for Erin. That was our first mistake, the second was sitting down at a table in the Busholm, and the third was ordering pitchers of Budweiser beer. After a substantial number of pitchers had satisfied our thirsts, our driver who remained sober enough (but just barely) navigated us back home. In truth none of us were feeling too sprightly by the time we got back to Orangeville. We were fortunate that the highway constabulary must have also been out celebrating with St. Patrick that night as well, otherwise our threesome would all likely still be in the hoosecow some fifty years later. As it was, the wife of one of our group (not me) reported that her husband who was dumped off on the front steps of their home, made it the last few yards on his hands and knees. I wasn't much better off! Fortunately we had the rest of the weekend to recover before returning to conduct our classes on Monday morning in prim and proper fashion, showing no obvious signs of our celebratory indiscretions. I haven't been able to look a bottle of Budweiser in the eye since.

My present day drinking habits see me usually nursing a twelve-pack of beer throughout a year if I even buy any beer at all. My preference used to be for Scotch such as J&B or Chivas Regal. The latest variety I purchased, sported the label 'SHEEP DIP,' 8-Year-old pure Malt Scotch Whisky, much enjoyed by the village of Oldbury-on-Severn) bottled in Edinburgh, Scotland. I enjoy the odd nip of Harvey's Bristol Cream, Irish Cream or perhaps Bushmills Irish whisky. While on a visit to Ireland, my brew of choice was a pint of dark-as-sin Guinness. Distillers will never get rich on my drinking habits, but who knows when the devil's brew might suddenly saturate my creative spirit and lead to more intoxicating prose? All questions about what effect my bouts with booze have had on my writing haven't been answered but perhaps after I've read the previously mentioned novel, Olivia Laing's tome *The Trip To Echo Spring,* reasons for my drinking binges may become more saturated with wisdom. My thoughts about writing under the influence suggest the quotation of author Tom Morris. "People suck the foam off the beer of life and never drink deeply of the real brew."

15 The School of Hard Knocks

"It is better to ask some of the questions than to know all of the answers." James Thurber

Once my seventeen years of formal education was nearly complete, I felt ready to educate the world. 1961 was an excellent year to consider entering the teaching business following my graduation from Queen's. From the large number of teaching positions being offered, I chose and was accepted by one in London, Ontario. Because I still had to complete teacher training, I registered for a summer course in London to complete my teaching qualifications. The London School Board had accepted my application to teach for them starting in September 1961, however, I received a surprise when I arrived to teach mathematics that first year. London Board Officials had assigned me to G.A. Wheable collegiate, not to Clark Road Collegiate, the one I'd signed to teach at originally. It was a surprise, but since I was entirely new, it didn't make much difference to me at the time. Wheable was located in a 'lower' working class section of London, whereas Clark Road was more attuned to the mucky muck status of society. Maybe it worked out better for me in the long run, who knows? My attitude was, c'est la vie, a job is a job. Looking back at my year at Wheable, I did make my share of mistakes but hopefully I learned from them. I probably wouldn't have wanted my kid to be in one of my classes that first year but we all have to start somewhere. I would classify year one as an opportunity to see how I might fare as a teacher, and get any first-year jitters under my belt but at least that first year was not a complete disaster.

Two incidents stick in my mind from that beginning year of teaching. During one class while a group of students was congregating around the pencil sharpener, ostensibly to sharpen pencils, one student suddenly crashed to the floor. When I looked into the eyes of this prone kid, I was looking at a pair of glassy eyeballs. Apparently one of his (friends?) had punched the downed kid in the solar plexus thus sending him to the floor as if he'd been pole axed. It was a minor incident, but one that taught me to be more wary at all times during classes.

The second incident was a case when I was taught a lesson by the students. I was supervising an absent teacher's class. Students, most of whom were on the low I.Q. scale, began asking questions related to a world map hanging on the wall at the front of the room. It was all a con job on their part. While my attention remained riveted on the map and their questions, I think several kids buggered-off from class without me realizing it. God knows what other antics might have been going on behind my back as well as I was being distracted?

In the beginning, at Wheable, I taught math principally to junior classes, marked tests and completed the usual teaching duties. I think I was so busy surviving my first year that little remains in my mind except those two incidents just described. I began to teach at age 22, resulting in several occasions when in classes I was expected to teach, there were students who were as old as, or older than I was. This made it more difficult to maintain discipline, but I managed! It seems hard to believe that my first year can be summed up in two incidents, one of my students getting punched in the gut, and me being made a fool of by a group of unwashed kids. Oh well, I guess that's just part of education, both theirs, and mine.

During my first year of teaching I had retired my Morris Minor convertible and replaced it with a Pontiac sedan, which although cheap and used had more going for it than the convertible did. On a weekend early in the school year, I had an opportunity to attend a pig roast in Brampton. Since my sister-in-law Joan worked at Peel Memorial hospital as a nurse, she arranged a blind date for me with Dorothy, a young lady working in the hospital lab. Imagine being a blind date at a pig roast! I learned after the event that at the time of the roast, I did not make a great hit with Dorothy, but I mustn't have turned out to be a complete loser as Dorothy was willing to go out with me on several occasions following that first date. I guess if the choice was between me and a roast pig, I won out. Our relationship blossomed from the pig roast to the extent that when I had finished teaching for a year in London, I decided that I would seek a new job in Brampton, thus cutting down my travelling time to meet with Dorothy on a regular basis. Consequently in 1962, the Peel County Board of Education hired me to teach at Central Peel Composite School on Kennedy Road in Brampton.

I rented a room in Brampton and spent that second summer attending the second half of my teaching course, this time in Toronto instead of London. At the end of the Toronto course, I would be fully qualified to teach high school mathematics after I took one more math course to upgrade my Queen's degree. I had no trouble completing that extra course, thus becoming fully qualified with a Specialist Degree in Mathematics.

I proposed to Dorothy on a Friday 13th (so my wife reminds me) and our wedding took place in the hamlet of Snelgrove on Highway #10 north of Brampton on Dec. 22/62.

Dorothy was Anglican, while my church of choice was United (although I seldom attended its services) and the minister who married us was Baptist (so it looks like we had all of our religious bases covered). The church where our wedding took place has since been taken over by the Coptic Orthodox Patriachate Archangel Michael and Saint Tekla Church, just to round off our religious connections further. Our wedding took place during the school Christmas holiday leaving us little time or cash for a honeymoon, except to visit friends in Willowdale.

There were a limited number of apartment buildings in Brampton, but we did rent suitable accommodations in Scottwood Towers, a reasonably respectable complex within walking distance of my new school and Dorothy's workplace at Peel Memorial Hospital. While I taught in Brampton, I continued to gain confidence and experience, partly from the students and by just being involved with the subject of mathematics. Most of my memories of teaching at Central Peel were related to my

relationships with helpful colleagues. Principal William McDowell was a fatherly figure with a thatch of thick silver hair. His two vice-principals were opposite in personalities. Art Martin, a portly chap with a build like Lou Costello, one of the partners of the Abbott & Costello comedy team. Art's genial nature was supplemented by the fact that he enjoyed a good cigar and stiff drink. His partner, Ken Dagg, dressed like a banker more than a school administrator. Ken always wore a three-piece suit and sported a gold watch chain across his chest. He was much more reserved than Art, but the two complemented one another and were a very effective pair. My department head, Bill Springle, was a balding experienced teacher always ready to offer advice whenever I needed it. Fellow teachers included George Inch, an ex-navy man, matronly Emily Fletcher, and good-natured Big Ron Davies.

My love life and being a new husband probably took precedence over my teaching during three years in Brampton, as I continued to mature as a mathematics teacher. One of the few memorable events associated with Brampton was historical and not mathematical. It was while seated in the Central Peel staff room that I learned of the assassination of US President John F. Kennedy.

Looking out of my classroom window, I looked down on the A&P parking lot, not a heartening sight compared to the rolling hills of Dufferin County to the North. With a Brampton growth spurt in the offing, I decided to seek a new position in Orangeville, a much smaller farm-related community. Once again, personality prevailed. Following a meeting with Orangeville High School principal Maurice Cline, I ended up in a new teaching position at a new school. I didn't realize when I signed on in 1965 that this would encompass the next thirty years of my educational career. Maurice Cline was a six foot six dynamo who left no doubt he was in charge. Maurice's belly laugh rumbled up from his size ten

Dacks, culminating in a ham-handed slap to his thigh. You could always be aware of him approaching in the halls. The clickers on his heels announced that he was coming, much like the clattering of shoes on a team of Clydesdales. Maurice could turn his hand to any task, and knew every student personally in his school. He had a heart of gold, and as long as you did the job expected of you, working with Maurice was great. Negotiating salary with him was a statement of fact, "I'll give you a hundred dollars more than anyone else!" That was it! I signed the contract. The only clearance left for me was to be approved by Maurice's wife Mary over one of her dinners.

My task in this memoir now is to sum up thirty years of teaching at Orangeville as succinctly and descriptively as possible. I began teaching mathematics but received a promotion to Department Head of Mathematics after a few years and remained in that position for perhaps another twenty. I received a second promotion to Program Supervisor of Pure Science. This last position placed me in charge of Mathematics, Chemistry, Physics, Biology, and Environmental Science. I felt comfortable in Math, Physics, and Chemistry, but had never studied Biology. The only way I could function effectively as Program supervisor was to depend on the expertise of Assistant Department Heads in each subject area. They had the knowledge and experience I didn't have. I then had two educational philosophies to deal with; one was teaching, while the other was administrative. As a supervisor, I kept departmental meetings to a minimum, listened to what subject teachers had to say, tried to keep everyone informed and made decisions only when I had considered all input. My philosophy always was 'let teachers teach.' I tried not to bog teachers down in demands from my seniors. Many times I ignored mandates passed down to me from the upper administration. I let teachers do their jobs and tried to keep them from being bugged by rules that I considered ridiculous. This practice never got me into trouble because often idiotic rules eventually just disappeared like a puff of smoke into the administrative mire. After several years I requested a return to my old Math Head job, and it was from that position that I retired in 1995, after thirty-four years of teaching (thirty in Orangeville).

During my thirty-four years of educational excellence, my duties were limited to teaching math classes until I arrived in Orangeville. There as a Department Head, I often participated in the hiring process, interviewing new prospective math teachers. One interesting result of this was the belief (so I found out later) that those doing the hiring often hired teachers like themselves. In spite of this belief, if it is in fact true, members of the math department tended to get along well together. Once new teachers were hired, I sometimes had to take them under my wing, helping them to adapt to their new jobs. One young teacher that we hired, Jim Lord, was a hippyish draft-dodger from the southern USA. He, and his hefty wife Beth, named their son "Love" and Beth's idea of suitable dress was a pair of baggy overalls. (Perhaps that was all she could afford at the time.)

It was often the case, in schools in general, that when time came to establish timetables in September, the principal would often assign teachers to classes which they were not fully qualified to teach. Excess bodies were too frequently 'dumped' into the math department where hopefully they could cope with a junior math class. In one instance, the administration gave a Grade Mine math class to a shop teacher. He couldn't cope, so the class went to a music teacher, who fared no better. The main problem was that the class would have been a handful, even for a fully qualified math teacher. The administration, in their wisdom, or lack thereof, solved the problem after three weeks, by foisting the class onto me. Even as an experienced teacher, I found the group to be a

challenge, particularly after they had established bad habits during
the weeks with previous teachers. I did survive that class for a
year, but it was a trying experience.

During my leisure time, I became involved in a variety of
artistic activities, with the result that I felt quite at home teaching
beginning art courses to grade nine students. To prevent a teacher
from being saddled with an art class that they weren't qualified to
teach when it came time to assign classes in September, I
volunteered to teach the odd art class myself. My out-of-school art
experience included, evening courses studying egg tempera
painting in Toronto and summer classes in life drawing. This was
all while I continued to submit editorial cartoons for publication in
the Orangeville Banner Newspaper, a practice that had begun in
1967 on a regular irregular basis. My cartoons did not go unnoticed

by my superiors in the county school board office. One of my
cartoons with an educational theme poked fun at my higher-ups, or
so they thought. The official who was the subject of the cartoon

wasn't pleased (to say the least) so I requested an interview with him to explain my view of humour. He wasn't impressed with what I had to say about the humour of the cartoon nor did I feel that I had done anything wrong.

After I left his office, the director sent his assistant superintendent around to figuratively rap my knuckles and tell me what a naughty act I'd performed. They requested that I write a letter of apology. I did so but found it extremely difficult to apologize without actually apologizing. The tempus in the teapot eventually settled down and I never lost my job (even though they threatened disciplinary action, whatever that was intended to mean). In November of 1977, I received the following letter addressed to me from the upper echelon.

Dear Mr. McCarthy:

"The political cartoon in the Orangeville Banner depicting the Chairman of the Board and the Director of Education in the manner in which you portrayed the men in regard to the issue at hand demonstrates, in my opinion:

(a) Unprofessional conduct
(b) An overwhelming lack of sensitivity for the issue and persons involved
(c) Extremely poor judgement.
    Behaviour of this nature will not be tolerated by members of the staff of the Dufferin County Board of Education and may lead to disciplinary action."

With the advancing pace of technology, the math department became responsible for Computer Science classes as well as mathematics. I enjoyed the logic involved in teaching computer programming but was uncomfortable with all of the computer hardware involved in the subject. I did not enjoy the fact that some of my students often knew more than I did about the mechanics of computers. Some kids spent hours at home playing with their computers so became well versed in screwing up our computer systems. The problems they created were usually a mystery to me. I just wasn't interested in spending the amount of time they did, so left the computer courses to teachers who expressed a wish to teach those particular classes.

As a department head, I had the opportunity to pick from a variety of professional development courses. A Thinking Skills course offered by Edward De Bono, the originator of the term 'lateral thinking' caught my attention. As a result of De Bono's presentation, I now own at least a dozen copies of his books on thinking skills. The book *Six Thinking Hats* is a particularly informative volume which has applications in the classroom as well as department administration. I thus became more interested in teaching thinking skills in conjunction with my mathematics classes. This began to affect my general philosophy of teaching. I never allowed students to laugh at another student who asked a question. As far as I was concerned, there was no such thing as a 'dumb' question. As a Chinese proverb once said, "He who asks, may be a fool for five minutes. He who doesn't is a fool for a lifetime." I always maintained that the only dumb question is the one that was never asked. Too often during my teaching I have observed that if one person asks a question, many others can learn from the questioner's answer. Students are often afraid to ask questions because they feel it makes them look silly. To this day, it never bothers me to ask questions if something is not clear. I might be thought of as dumb, but who cares? At least I will be more likely to understand what is going on. On days before holidays, I often incorporated one of Edward De Bono's exercises into my classes. I would show students an item such as a golf ball or ruler, then ask them to give me as many uses for the item that they can think of. I emphasized the fact that no suggestion can be wrong or foolish. Any answer was possible. The amazing fact I discovered was that once I removed the chance of failure (a wrong answer) even the supposedly bonehead kid would come up with amazing uses for some items. There was one instance when a youngster suggested fitting roller blades with balls, like bearings, instead of wheels. I heard exactly the same suggestion from an engineer one year later while my wife and I were on our way to Florida. One of the interesting things about teaching in general is that you are never sure what students are learning from you. Often what they learn is not what you actually set out to teach to them thus teaching by example is likely one of the best tactics. Meeting with students after they have graduated is often very revealing as to how effective your teaching actually was. In addition to De Bono's thinking skills, I also pursued and still at times use mind maps as designed by author and thinker Tony Buzan.

Mr. John Asher, Principal of Orangeville District Secondary School completed my last teaching report in June of 1988. A portion of that report reads as follows:

"If Clare McCarthy was a horse, I would say that he was sound. Mr. McCarthy is an extremely effective and professional teacher, well respected by his students for his knowledge of mathematics, his pedagogical expertise and his rapport with students. A hallmark of his teaching is the classroom climate that he cultivates, one that is comfortable and nurturing while intellectually demanding. Students know they must come prepared to learn with the necessary materials, prepared assignments and intent to learn, and they do come prepared. Discipline, of course, is not a problem in this environment. He exhibits a warm, positive cooperative and at times light hearted demeanour and students respond in kind. His lesson objectives are clearly understood and appreciated . . . Mathematical concepts are clearly presented and firmly reinforced with numerous examples: few if any students could fail to grasp the essential ideas with such support."

I do not object to John Asher comparing me to a horse, in fact I considered my teaching methods as being thorough and demanding, as I tried to instill an atmosphere of warmth with an undercurrent of humour. Most classes responded to this approach while others required a firmer hand to ensure that things did not get out of control. I didn't consider myself to be a flashy teacher. I always gave examples early in a lesson covering topics prior to where I thought students might experience difficulties with concepts. All in all, I enjoyed my thirty-four years of teaching and was not one of those people who did not enjoy their chosen line of work. Teaching was great, but the administrative side of the job was often a major pain in the backside.

As a kid, and until I reached my late teens, I always had plenty of physical activity to keep myself in good shape, but by the age of approximately twenty-five, when I arrived in Orangeville to teach, I found it necessary to broaden my choice of physical activities to include walking, snowshoeing, and cross-country skiing. I tried downhill skiing, but chose to focus on the more leisurely cross-country version or snowshoeing when I could explore my surroundings in detail and focus on photographing winter landscapes. For several years I pursued Judo with Bob Ronson in Kitchener, rising to the lofty height of a yellow belt (the second from the bottom). Friends might suggest that yellow was the colour of the belt to which my character was most suited. I studied Daoist tai chi at the school in the Hockley Valley, then continued with Yang style tai chi under the guidance of Ed Boates at the High School in Orangeville during evenings. It was from my reading related to tai chi that I learned about the concept of 'wu wei,' 'to do without doing.' I always considered this epitomized the leisurely way my father led his life, and it is one that I hoped to emulate.

During my Orangeville days, I spent a good deal of time hiking on the Bruce Trail through the Hockley Valley. It was during this time I purchased Mirk, a Border Collie pup to accompany me on these walks. Mirk was by far, smarter than I was and on any of my walks alone or later with French chef Pierre Oger, Mirk would cover many times the distance that Pierre and I rambled. On several outings in the Hockley Valley, we encountered a naked hiker and I even managed to capture a photograph of the bare buttocks of the streaking hiker as his bare bum bounced into the distance. Unfortunately Mirk developed a stomach tumour in his sixth year forcing me to have a vet end his life. Pierre and I scattered Mirk's cremated ashes along trails where he had previously enjoyed running.

I earlier discussed our religious connections related to the time when Dorothy and I were married by a Baptist minister. Although I was baptized as a teenager into the United Church, I seldom attended their services with the exception of a few occasions in Kingston, but while in Orangeville I did flirt briefly with the Buddhist religion at the temple on the way to Alton. I attended a few of their introductory classes, but didn't continue with the practice. Of all of the religions to which I've been exposed over the years, Buddhism is the one that comes closest to my preferred religious leanings. All religions have some good to offer, so I guess I just cherry pick the best of each, after all, they say there's only one God! When the late folksinger, activist Pete Seeger was asked about religion and his spiritual views, he replied, "I feel most spiritual when I'm out in the woods. I feel part of nature, looking up at the stars. (I used to say) I was an atheist. Now I say, it's all according to your definition of God. According to my definition of God, I'm not an atheist. Because I think God is everything. Whenever I open my eyes I'm looking at God, and whenever I'm listening to something I'm listening to God."

I tend to echo Seeger's idea of religion and his definition of God. A philosophy shared with Aldous Huxley, "My father considered a walk among the mountains as equivalent to church going."

As a result of my cycling accident, I took a break from teaching for a complete year. Other members of the staff of Orangeville High School temporarily took over my tasks until the end of my year of recovery, after which I returned to my old teaching position and job as department head. I experienced some minor problems adjusting back to work but still had the mental capacity to teach advanced calculus classes along with an assortment of other grades.

My cycling mishap was likely the watershed moment in my life. Foolishly, after the accident I had to prove to myself that I was still able to accomplish as many of the activities as I could previously. To this end, I purchased a Bluewater nylon canoe in Guelph and with Bob Ronson portaged into remote Blind Lake near Elliott Lake in Northern Ontario. We spent two weeks tenting, fishing and canoeing. Even though my right shoulder was separated as a result of the accident, and still is, I was able to hold my own paddling and on portages of the canoe on that trip.

16 Off to the Amazon Jungle

After testing my physical endurance through the Blind Lake canoe trip, I decided to up the ante gambling with my conditioning by embarking on a trip to the Amazon Jungle. This was an experience that I'd often considered, but finally decided, "The time has arrived." Great Expeditions was the name of the Vancouver Company which organized the trip. One attraction of the expedition was the possibility of viewing anacondas, giant python-like water snakes that often hung down from trees in the jungle so in the summer of 1984 I began making plans. From the Simcoe County Health Unit, I received a yellow fever shot and prescriptions for Chloraquin and Fansidar to prevent contracting malaria. The Health Unit also provided me with an information sheet on snake bites. I learned such comforting facts as, "cobras, mambas, tiger snakes and coral snakes have short unmoving fangs and the main action of their venom was neurotoxic, while rattlesnakes, Fer-de-lance and Mayan pit vipers have a small heat-sensitive pit between eye and nostrils. With these facts filed away in my recently scrambled brain, I completed my travel arrangements which included health insurance with a clause providing for the return shipping of my deceased carcass back to civilization in the event I succumbed to some malady or unexpected accident while out of the country.

I flew from Toronto to Miami via Air Canada, then by Equatoriana Airline, stopping first at Guyaquil on Ecuador's coast. As the aircraft settled onto the Guyaquil runway, I likened it to a great prehistoric bird settling into a primeval swamp. After loading freight and more passengers, we continued on to Quito, the country's capital. Quito sits at an altitude of 2,850 metres, in the Andes Mountains, 25 km from the equator. Travel books warn that because of the altitude, visitors might initially feel some discomfort. There are also increased effects of the sun at that height with the result that car dashboards sometimes crack from the heat.

Members of the travel company met our group of eight at the airport and took us to assign rooms at the Inca Imperial Hotel, and that evening we ventured out to find an eating establishment. Those who chose fried chicken discovered signs of a few pin feathers of the bird still remaining in the barbequed wings. We spent several days resolving lost luggage problems, a task which was made more complicated due to language difficulties. I had learned a bit of rudimentary Spanish, so was able to order two eggs (dos huevos) and a cold beer (cerveza frio), but not both for breakfast. Great Expeditions provided a guided tour of Quito and treated us to an impressive meal at a local restaurant. One evening while walking about town, we viewed protestors burning rubber tires out in the street and on another occasion a mobile water cannon in support of the visit of an American official was visible near government buildings.

After two days in Quito we boarded a dilapidated coach to cover a 360 mile trip climbing to 12,000 feet across the Andes Mountains via Tumbaco Valley where there had been snowstorms weeks before in some of these mountain passes. The rough gravel roads, with unguarded edges was not an experience for the faint of heart. We stopped for a swim at Papallacta hot springs where the water travelled underground from Reventador volcano, and breakfast was served at the Oro Negro Restaurant along the route. The name Oro Negro (Black Gold) suited our destination, the oil mining town of Lago- Agrio. The maitre'd of the restaurant was a mangy hound lying across the entrance way and the garbage disposal unit was a fat pig rooting around a side entrance. There was a picnic lunch stop to view "Las Catarates de San Rafael" waterfall before arriving in the town of Lago-Agrio which travel information described as the centre of different oil companies and the main trading town for the surrounding Indian tribes, (the Cofans, Secoyas and Sinas) who live along the Aquarico River.

We finally arrived in Lagio-Agrio at our hotel the Residencial Mexicana, which I would classify as 'seedy,' to be kind. Dave Wilford from Toronto shared a room with me. A mosquito net (containing several holes) hung over the bed, and we entertained ourselves by betting on several cockroaches racing around the door frame. A single light bulb hanging from the ceiling illuminated cracked walls and water stained wallpaper. As you might expect, there was no electronic entertainment such as a radio or TV set. Our evening meal was a buffet (of sorts) at a local restaurant where we met our jungle guide, Peter Buhl, who was also the owner of a steak house in Quito. Peter spoke English, Spanish and German, as well as a smattering of Indian dialects. Following that meeting, the local police arrested two members of our group. Gord Nagy and Francisco Beluse who were wearing camouflage clothing and were thought to be terrorists who had infiltrated the town from the surrounding jungle. Peter Buhl intervened and after the lads changed their clothing they were allowed to go free.

In spite of cockroaches and thoughts of malaria-carrying mosquitoes I slept soundly until the following morning when a rooster next door in a tin shed sounded our wakeup call. We showered under a trickle of rusty water in a washing area down the hall then headed for breakfast at 7:30 at the local cafeteria. Stepping outside in the morning was like walking into a sauna.

We traveled by coach to the river port of Aquarico to pick up our water transportation. The group organizers had ordered only one motorized canoe, but our numbers had increased to fourteen so we needed another vessel. After some protracted negotiations, Peter finally arranged for a second canoe. Both canoes were carved from single trees and holes were patched hither and yon by bits of what looked like tin from soup cans, or the like. To modify one of the seats, a crewman whacked off the end of a chunk of wood with a machete, and wedged the board into place between the sides of the canoe thus providing another seat. Outboard motors powered both vessels but one canoe was covered by a sheet of tin serving as a roof providing protection from the sun and rain.

At our first stop for the evening at the Secoya Indian village of San Pablo, inhabited by approximately 150 natives, I bought two feathered necklaces for approximately fifty cents each from a toothless old lady. Any of the spots where we stopped for the night usually contained an open thatched hut built by oil prospectors who had previously passed through the area. We slung hammocks from the rafters and with only one thin blanket I spent comfortable nights sleeping. Since I had never previously slept in a hammock, I had expected that I would be uncomfortable, but that was not the case. At one site several days later, the hut had been used for preparing meals thus small bits of food were left in cracks in the floor. The location seemed to be ideal, but after we had hung up our hummocks and it became dark, cockroaches emerged. An army of gleaming eyes was the most obvious sign of the number of cockroaches that came out of hiding. I made sure my bag was well zipped and applied Muskol insect repellant to the support ropes on my hammock to discourage the roaches from disturbing my sleep that night. It was with some sense of relief that we departed that area the next day.

Following one of the days of meandering down the Aquarico River, Peter suggested that we go for a swim in a nearby spot where I decided to leave my shoes on. After swimming, when

I reached the shore, and was climbing out of the water, Peter suggested that wearing my shoes was a good idea, because sting rays tended to bury themselves in the muddy bottom. Stepping on these creatures could give you a nasty wound from the barb mounted in a sting ray's tail. I failed to see how my sandals would provide any protection to such an injury, so I felt relieved to climb ashore without having had to contend with one of these aquatic creatures. On several other occasions, we swam with a bar of soap in a freshwater lake after a grubby day of travelling. I have yet to know why attacks, by piranha fish, were never a threat to us bathers at such times. Often the canoes would encounter sunken logs blocking our path in the river, forcing a crew member to climb onto the log which would sink the log further, as he worked the canoe across it. On other occasions a sandbar in the river would hinder the canoe's progress. I was one of the ones who would hop overboard wearing shorts and sandals with water up to my arse as I worked the canoe past the sand bar to freedom further down the river.

We carried all of our food supplies for ten days aboard the canoes and two plastic barrels kept supplies such as bread and toilet paper dry during our travels. Breakfast often consisted of bread, cheese, jam and fried bananas, but Packo the cook, provided some interesting meals using a gas ring and tank of propane. Whenever we camped, Packo would trot down to the river with an aluminum pail to scoop up water. After boiling the water for a minimum of ten minutes, he would declare it suitable for drinking or for use to make tea or coffee. One of the local Indians, Vittoriano, a native approximately sixty years of age, accompanied us on the trip as a resource person. He demonstrated how to construct a thatched roof and when we expressed an interest in fishing, he used his machete to hack off tree limbs to provide us with fishing poles. Vittoriano attached a piece of line to each limb, then a chunk of wire as a leader, and finally a hook. Since we would be fishing for piranhas, the wire leader was to prevent our catch from chomping with its sharp teeth through the line. Vittoriano indicated that when fishing for piranha, we should stick the end of the pole into the water and thrash it around. This would attract the fish hopefully making them believe that some edible quarry had fallen into the water. The day we went in the canoe fishing for piranha, it was my responsibility to place all of our catches on a forked stick by inserting the stick through the fish's gills. As I stood in the bottom of the canoe in my flip-flops, caught piranhas thrashed around on the bottom of the canoe until I held them safely on my forked stick. I can recall one person shouting, "Watch your feet Mac!" This was a completely redundant comment to make with my bare feet exposed to gnashing teeth! That evening Packo prepared a tasty piranha soup for dinner using the two dozen or so fish that we had caught. I can still recall the look on the face of a young lad from Ottawa who pulled out and held up a six-inch long intact piranha backbone from his soup. Whenever we fished for piranha, Vittoriano usually began with a tiny piece of cloth for a lure, but once he caught the first fish, he would cut it into small pieces to use as bait for further attempts.

To supplement our supplies, at strategic spots along the river, Peter bartered for bananas and papaya from natives in thatched huts on stilts and since we had no refrigeration on the trip, one of the transported items was a live chicken for our meal at the end of the expedition. On that occasion, Packo terminated the unlucky bird's life and using the carcass he brewed a delicious chicken stew.

To answer the call of nature during the trip was another challenge. Periodically we would encounter a pit in the ground covered by logs with an opening spot in the centre. Positioning one's backside over the hole, then doing your business, was like trying to thread a needle with your behind. In cases of emergency, one would usually just locate the most convenient isolated piece of shrubbery and with no toilet paper available a hand-full of leaves would have to do the job. One had to exercise caution that the leaves being used were not already inhabited by some tiny jungle beasties.

Peter Buhl usually wore a Boy Scout-style hat, shorts and a T-shirt, but at times no shirt at all. He very much resembled Harrison Ford as Indiana Jones in the Raiders of the Lost Ark. While on the river one day, Peter had to extract a thorn from his right bicep after a brush with a branch of prickly vegetation. During one outing when we caught a tiger fish, it became clear that most fish in that jungle area were well equipped with a good set of nasty-looking teeth. Our group spent several days camped near freshwater Lake Cuyano where we were able to swim and fish. One morning after we got up, one young lad caught a giant black widow spider on the floor of the hut. He kept it in a bottle to take home, but I doubt that it ever got that far. On one occasion, a couple of the lads attempted to brew a narcotic drink from a sample of vegetation that they had discovered, but the brew only served to make the experimenters throw up. We took a few walks into the jungle with Vittoriano, but considering we were up to our arses in water at times, it wasn't exactly a 'walk in the park,' even though our guide threw in a few logs to walk on so we would not sink out of sight. Vittoriano often acted like a kid, swinging like Tarzan on vines. He was one tough old guy walking through the jungle in his bare feet. Once hospitalized with an appendix attack for a few days, he couldn't stand being confined, so he checked himself out of the hospital and headed back to the jungle. One young native kid in the camp had a pet pig which he kept like a puppy on a piece of twine. The piglet escaped one day and headed out into the water. I didn't realize that pigs were such great swimmers. Vittoriano hopped into a motorized canoe to chase and round up the swimming piglet and return it to the young lad.

At the end of our stay in Cuyabend National park, we headed upstream via the Aguas Negras River where we got caught in a torrential downpour with rain coming down in sheets. We dried out at a native family's bamboo hut with a thatched roof and had a meal of bananas and freshly cooked tapir or capybara before continuing our journey upstream to Tarapoa where we disembarked to take land transportation to Lago-Agrio for a flight over Cayambe volcano back to Quito, thus ending our Amazon Headwaters expedition.

Since I had come such a long distance to get from Orangeville to Ecuador, I decided to stay an additional week in Quito at the Inca Imperial hotel before heading back home. During that time, I meandered around Quito shopping, enjoying the sights, and trying out my Spanish, with varying degrees of success. I purchased a native doll for our daughter, Margaret Anne, a silver bracelet for my wife Dorothy, and an imitation shrunken head, a wooden carved bust and a blowgun with darts for myself. I got lost at least once which forced me to take a cab back to the hotel. For drinks I stuck to cold beer, which I knew how to order in Spanish. Bottled water was available but tap water was not drinkable, as one of the lads found out after developing a case of the runs and vomiting. I experimented with my newly purchased blowgun in my hotel room and was able to propel a dart far enough to strike the wall at the other side of the room. Not exactly deadly accuracy! The fluffy kapok on the end of the dart, seals the tube, thus forcing the dart out through the weapon's barrel after a hearty puff. My roommate accompanied me by bus on a day trip to the Otovallo native market. To entertain passengers during the trip, the bus driver played loud raucous Spanish music over the sound system. I took a good many 35 mm slides in the jungle and at the market, where I was able to view a cockfight in progress. It was not my idea of wholesome family entertainment as the fighting roosters fitted with spurs attempted to tear each other to shreds.

When I reached Toronto by air, one of my bags was still in Miami. On a second trip to Toronto airport to retrieve my lost luggage, customs officials informed that my blowgun was a prohibited weapon, which I couldn't bring into the country however they did allow me to keep the darts and the rest of my souvenirs. I should have kicked up a stink over the blowgun, and claimed it was for educational use! As it turned out, some lousy customs agent likely has my blowgun mounted on his basement recreation room wall. All in all, I passed my personal physical test with flying colours and no ill effects, coming home with a collection of slides and precious memories. I also discovered a few dead cockroaches in my suitcase, much to the chagrin of my wife. And no! We didn't encounter any anacondas hanging from the trees, but we did spot many Caymans, colourful birds, monkeys and wild turkeys during the trip.

As a result of my bicycle accident I received a financial settlement from the insurance company of the lady who ran into me. This settlement allowed me to bankroll a continuation of my peripatetic ways and it also permitted us to pay off the mortgage on our newly purchased bungalow in Orangeville.

If I was to offer any practical advice about travel in this memoir, it might be: If you harbour any inclination to explore the world, do not leave it until you are too old to physically cope with planned trips. For me, my optimum age was forty.

Any trips which I made by myself were definitely not comfortable package tours. Most involved fairly rough conditions much like camping. After returning from a successful Amazon Headwaters trip, I felt that I'd been seriously bitten by the travel bug and as a result of my accident settlement I could afford to expand my travel plans. Thus in 1985, I sought to keep on the move by signing up for a Kenya photo safari as offered by 'I'm Proud To Be Me,' a company in Toronto. The main attraction as advertised by the tour company was an opportunity to photograph wild animals in their natural setting on the Serengeti Plains as well as viewing the annual migration of wildebeests with professional photographic Fred Donner as the photographic resource person on the trip.

After landing in Nairobi, we were to begin our safari experience following a stop at Africana Sea Lodge in Mombasa, a Moorish settlement on the shore of the Indian Ocean. The following story 'Mombasa Morning' is a slightly fictionalized version of my one and only deep sea fishing opportunity. Although I fictionalized the incident and names, all events were based on what actually happened.

Mombasa Morning

"I wasn't much of a fisherman. I'd be the first to admit that." As a kid with freckles and flaming red hair, I'd used a dime-store rod and reel to land a few unfortunate sunfish and catfish that proved to be in the wrong place at the wrong time. My largest catch was a motley old carp measuring three feet in length. It had been spawning in the shallow waters and reed beds of the muddy Grand River near my home, but I must confess that I used a length of two by four to club this monster into submission. Of course these are not tales about which true fishermen would boast. A real aficonado would describe encounters with stupendous aquatic giants that put up tremendous battles before slipping away to freedom in the murky depths.

In spite of my pathetic fishing record established during my youth, the year I signed up for a trip to Africa with a select group of adventurers, I knew that I'd have the opportunity to erase my reputation as a less than expert angler. On our way with the Great Adventure Travel Company to photograph wildlife in Kenya, our group aboard an aging KLM747 landed first in Nairobi. We then piled into safari vans for our journey to Mombasa, on the shore of the Indian Ocean.

The options offered to us during our stay at Mombasa's Jadini Beach the following day included sightseeing or deep-sea-fishing. My logical choice was fishing, but there was an expectation that those wishing to participate in that event would share all additional costs equally.

The day before that morning when my fishing reputation was sure to be revitalized, I spent the afternoon swinging in a rattan hammock buffeted by gentle sea breezes. Between snoozes, I squinted through shimmering heat waves rippling off the pristine beach sands. A native fisherman in a primitive dhow stabilized by two outriggers attached by lengths of rusty wire was faintly visible just off shore. I watched the lone occupant maneuver his craft carved from the trunk of a mango tree, and smiled as I dreamed confidently that my return from the next day's fishing expedition would be like Ernest Hemingway's hero in The Old Man And The Sea, coming back to shore with a giant fish in tow.

When I arrived at the beach the following morning to meet my fishing companions, I had second thoughts about my choice when I discovered that due to fatigue, upset stomachs, and a general lack of interest in fishing, our numbers were reduced to three. My sole companions for the event were professional photographer Fred Droner (affectionately known as Freddie the Flash) and Big Dave Dawson, one of the owners of the Great Adventure Travel Company. Although the reduced size of the party meant that my wallet would be whacked harder than I'd expected, I figured the experience would be well worth any additional dent it might put in my budget

A thirty-five foot vessel silhouetted against the fiery glow of a rising tropical sun, wallowed drunkenly as it tugged at its restraining anchor. With footwear removed, our trio sloshed through hip-deep water toward the vessel, the *Rosie-B*. We were lugging our day's supplies of several cases of soft drinks, snacks and an extra large case of Tusker beer. Assisted by the crew's helping hands, we clambered up the ship's boarding ladder and were welcomed with the traditional Swahili greeting, "Jambo Bwana." Our Captain, John Bland, was a salty British ex-navy man who addressed his native crew in Swahili, interspersed frequently with four-letter English expletives. The captain's ebony-skinned daughter, Rose, greeted us with a flashing ivory smile as expansive as a piano keyboard, while Hondo, the young native deckhand, skittered crablike around the vessel, tending to the captain's departure orders.

Once we'd settled aboard ship, a pair of Evinrude outboards coughed to life and fired the vessel through a break in the reef running parallel to the shore. My knuckles whitened as I gripped the arms of my chair, and with engines throbbing and propellers vibrating, we lurched over plumes of white foam generated by waves crashing against the reef. When I expressed my concern about the turbulence, Captain John calmly informed me the sea that morning was, "as smooth as a duck's arse!" In my estimation we were soon travelling at a velocity suitable only for catching flying fish, but eventually the vessel settled down to a much more reasonable speed.

The crew baited six trolling lines, Dave baited Fred, and I planned my strategy. Fred, Dave, and I drew lots to see who would cast out the first line. As usual, I lost, but being the gracious hosts, Fred agreed with Dave that I should be Numero Uno at testing my luck. I was convinced that rather than just being polite, they really wanted me to be first so they could copy my technique. As soon as I was seated and the crew buckled me in, my first objective was to get the feel of the rod and reel. After I made several tentative attempts to rewind my line, Captain John leaned over my shoulder and muttered, "Sir, this is not a winch!" With those words of advice, I tried to make my line retrieval less winch-like (whatever that was) and did manage to land a Cravalle weighing in at about ten pounds. The captain gaffed the fish and dragged it flopping across the deck. It wasn't quite in Hemingway's league, but we all have to start somewhere.

I relinquished the rod and reel to Dave and retired to the upper deck to celebrate my achievement. Rapidly downing a jar of Tusker beer, was not the wisest act to perform on the upper deck of a wildly rolling ship. My rate of consumption of the effervescent brew was exceeded only by the rate at which bubbles from the consumed beverage escaped through my nostrils. A quick trip to the ship's railing provided some relief for my queasiness and then I collapsed into a deck chair to await my next turn at winching in another mystery catch (barracuda, marlin or whatever it might be). The fishing expedition ended sooner than I would have liked and as the *Rosie-B* approached the beach, Hondo tossed a four-pronged grappling anchor overboard. He was slightly premature in performing this task with the result that the still-moving vessel struck one of the anchor prongs thereby punching a hole in the ship's side. Needless to say, Captain John was not amused. Since we'd finished the case of Tusker Beer, our trio's departure from the *Rosie-B* was relatively painless. Through my fuzzy brain, my last recollections are of the crew bailing feverishly to keep ahead of the leak. Much like the proverbial rats, our threesome skipped ashore with our catch. As we scampered up the beach toward the lodge, we could hear Captain John still issuing orders in Swahili, interspersed with new English expletives, ones I'd never heard before.

The *Rosie-B* returned from the trip with a bounty of one Kingfish and six Cravalles, two of which were mine. After Chef Gordon of the African Sea Lodge barbecued our haul for the group's evening meal, I felt I could finally attach that elusive term, "accomplished angler" to my name.

On any future occasions when my fishing buddies trumpet about "the one that got away" I could conveniently forget about catching lousy sunfish, catfish, or even the motley carp, and instead boast about, "My monstrous Cravalles that fed the multitude at the African Sea Lodge in the Indian Ocean port of Mombasa."

Following our stay at Africana Sea Lodge on Diani beach, we headed out by safari van to the following stops on our photographic tour:

VOI SAFARI LODGE "In Tsvo East National Park. Located on top of a large cliff. Fantastic view for miles. Watch elephant, buffalo, lion and numerous other animals approach waterholes at base of cliff. Viewing hide located at waterholes, which are floodlit at night."

NGULIA SAFARI LODGE "Tsavo West National Park. Located on the edge of Ndowe Escarpment. Every room has a balcony and overlooks a waterhole. Frequented by elephants which rub against the main patio wall. Lots of birds. Fantastic sunrises. The view is a photographer's dream with floodlit waterholes."

KILAGUNI LODGE "Tsavo West National Park. Great view of snowcapped Mt. Kilimanjaro (19,300 ft.) and many lesser volcanoes. Occasionally the elusive leopard or lions make kills at one of its numerous waterholes which are renowned for vast herds of buffalo and elephant."

"I told you we were too close!"

AMBOSELI LODGE Amboseli National Park. "Fantastic view of Mt. Kilimanjaro. Dusty and hot is the park but it is famous for its lions, elephants, cheetah and black rhino. A birder's paradise at Lake Kiuko."

LAKE NAIVASHA LODGE "Lake Naivasha is situated among giant fever trees, manicured lawns and exotic flowers. Take a water boat tour of the lake and see hippos, darters, heron and assorted aquatic birdlife."

KEEKOROK LODGE "Masai Mara Game reserve. Lions, buffalo, and the migration at your doorstep. Thousands of zebra, wildebeasts, giraffe and topi.

A BIG MAC ATTACK

Hyena, leopard, cheetah and hunting dogs search the plains for prey. Black rhino and roan antelope are also to be found, as well as birds which are found everywhere. Animals roam the lodge at night under flood lights."

LAKE NAKARU HOTEL "Lake Nakaru National Park. Flamingos by the hundreds of thousands aquatic birds, hippos, the rothchilds giraffe."

THE ARK "Aberdares National Park. Located in the famous salient area of Aberdares National Park. The leopard and the elusive shy bongo and forest elephants are often found at the ARK`s floodlit salt lick. Many forest dwelling birds are found here. Built in the shape of a huge ark."

TREETOPS "Aberdares National Park. 'Where a princess became Queen Elizabeth II' Built in the branches of a large cape chestnut tree overlooking the waterhole and salt lick. Laugh at the antics of baboons stealing human's tea-time cakes and laugh at wart hogs feuding."

NORFOLK HOTEL "Marks the end of the Kenya safari trip."

I accumulated a vast number of photographic slides featuring lions, elephants, wildebeests, vultures feeding on animal kills, flamingos, sunsets, dancing Masai warriors and as broad a spectrum of wildlife as I could capture. During the safari, one member of the group organized a daily diary of events and asked each participant to contribute towards the diary. I have included in this memoir the drawings that I presented to her.

Following this trip, I obtained zoom lenses for two Kodak projectors along with a device to provide music and fade slides in and out. On a number of occasions I presented evenings of armchair travel for night school programs operated by the Toronto Board of Education. Along with synchronized music to the slides, I presented a verbal commentary then answered questions. These presentations were based on my trips to the Amazon, Kenya, Iceland, Patagonia the Canadian Arctic, the Seychelles, and Ste. Pierre & Miquelon.

During this time in the 1980s I was a member of the Orangeville camera club. This allowed me to increase my photographic knowledge from seminars and tips from other more experienced photographers. Since meetings were held in the evenings at Orangeville District Secondary School, I got roped into serving as the club's president for a number of years. The main reason I lasted almost ten years as president was because members were content to let me shoulder the load, but after a few years, I bailed out and left members to carry on with someone else at the helm.

17 Land of Ice and Fire

On Friday July 3, 1987, I departed from Toronto via an Air Canada 727 on a flight to La Guardia Airport in New York. We bussed to JFK Airport then took an Icelandic Air DC8 to Reykjavik, Iceland. The DC8's flying time was 4 hours and 50 minutes. Iceland is a land of contrasts with glaciers geysers greenery, rock, rock, and more rock broken by numerous waterfalls. The centre of the island is largely uninhabited with most of the population gathered around the coast due to ease of transportation by boat. The centre of the island is open for travel only about six weeks of the year. When I arrived by air, I likened the area to the way Sudbury used to look years ago. One of the most unexpected features of Iceland was the length of daylight. It was possible to take photographs almost any time at night. A good many of my slides featured textures, fishing nets and birds such as puffins as well as boats and their amazing reflections. For all of the trips that I've been on, I keep a travel diary describing activities each day. The diary helps me at times like this recalling events that I might have otherwise forgotten. In my collection of Iceland slides, I have a number from a visit to a whaling station where workers sliced whale meat and blubber. If memory serves me correctly, there was quite a stench in the air, but I have no record of that stop in my notes.

After I returned home, I composed a slide presentation of my trip and invited my roommate Wayne on the trip over to view the slides. Although Wayne was with me during most of my picture taking, he kept saying, "I don't remember that!" I guess one of the big benefits gained from photography is that one tends to become more observant as I particularly appreciate small details such as texture, reflections etc. It seems that some folks don't really notice a lot of what goes on in life. At one point during my Icelandic trip, I reckoned that I'd taken approximately 1,000 slides which was about half of my supply.

While in Reykjavik, we visited a pub, where the entertainer was Johnny King, a country singer. Johnny was also a church deacon in a town further north where he also led the church choir. At the pub, I purchased a cassette tape by country singer Hallbjorn Hjartarson who performed such classics as 'Sveitadrengurinn' which translates as 'The country boy,' plus the heart rending tune, 'Solskinsbrusid' which locals might recognize as 'A Sunny Smile.' It is intriguing listening to a bouncy country and western tune in Icelandic. I purchased many tapes of Icelandic folk singing and passed them on to fellow teacher Slade Willis in Orangeville who sent on copies to his Icelandic relatives living around Winnipeg. Before the trip, while I was in Canada, I bought (but seldom used) an *Icelandic Encyclopedia* and the book, *How to Teach Yourself Icelandic*. All in all, Iceland was a most unusual country with a landscape very much like Ste. Pierre & Miquelon off the coast of Newfoundland. A fascinating part of travel is the people I met on the way, for example, on the flight to Iceland I chatted with 81 year old Al Crossland from Prescott. He climbed half way up Kilimanjaro at the age of 79, so I guess there's still hope for me yet.

18 Into the Land of Big Feet

In December of 1988, as a Christmas present to myself, I decided to spend Christmas Day at Estancia Christina an abandoned sheep ranch located in Patagonia, in southern Argentina. The following story documents that experience:

Patagonia was a land of contrasts. Its mountains, polar and glacial ice, coarse yellow pampas grass, and treeless arid desert all pointed to an extremely harsh environment. The bulk of Patagonia lies in Argentina east of the Andes, and refers to the whole of the mainland of south America south of latitude 40 degrees south. The name Patagonia is derived from the word, "Patagones" or big feet, a nickname given to the aboriginal Indians by early explorers. To quote explorer, Eric Shipton, "Lago Argentino, the land's main body of water resembled a giant squid with eight channels extending like sinuous tentacles penetrating deep into the foothills of the Andes."

My Christmas destination, the remote Estancia Christina was accessible from the mainland only by boat or overland on horseback. From the port of Punta Bandera on Lago Argentino, our chartered motor launch navigated into the north-channel via the narrow Hell's Gate passage. During this voyage, the Upsala Glacier cast off a gallery of fantastic translucent royal blue sculptures and as the icebergs passed our vessel, the bergs undulated responding to the whim of current and gale force winds. Our journey ended after approximately six hours at a rustic wooden dock which materialized like a mirage out of the mist. This marked our arrival at Estancia Christina, Patagonia's most remote habitation.

With their son Herbert, a couple, the Masters, emigrated in 1905 from England, and established a sheep ranch Estancia Christina named after their daughter who died when she was still a young girl. This estancia at one time was the grazing home for the Masters' 12,000 sheep. Since it took approximately 4 acres to raise one sheep, I conservatively estimated the area of La Christina to be 50,000 acres

In the 1940s and 50s, with the advent of synthetic fibres, and the declining market for mutton, raising sheep became no longer economically practical. At the time of my visit to the ranch, daughter-in-law, Jean Masters, by herself owned and operated all of this vast area. The 78 year-old widow was no longer interested in raising sheep and instead offered her ranch to host according to her, "naturalists, photographers, and people with energy and enthusiasm and respect for exploration and adventure in wild places."

From the wooden dock where our launch dropped anchor, our group of photographers followed the rough trail across rocky ground to a gate in a white weathered picket fence which surrounded a tiny house with a corrugated rusty iron roof. From the time she met us at the gate, Jean Masters wore a broad smile which continued to light up her face as she then herded our group into her spotless dining room. As we sat around her shiny red dining room table, Jean served mugs of steaming Argentine coffee and generous slices of freshly baked bread.

Following our welcoming snack, Jean darted about the house with the agility of a person half her age as she assigned cots for our sleeping bags. Our daily routine in the morning began first with a visit to the privy located conveniently outside the back door. Since there was no running water in the house, an enamel wash basin was located outside on a stand on the lawn. A pitcher of cold water was available for an invigorating early morning scrub. If that didn't wake you up, the cool breeze streaming down from the surrounding snowcapped peaks certainly would. Following breakfast with Jean, each of us prepared our own lunch so we could enjoy the rest of the day exploring the estancia in search of suitable subjects to photograph.

Rain barrels collected rainwater from the house's eaves, but usually whenever Jean's drinking water supply needed to be replenished, one member of our group would volunteer to trudge with a 5-gallon pail down to a nearby river. A giant water wheel moaned and groaned as it performed its task of scooping water from the river to fill the volunteer's waiting bucket. Since Jean's water wheel supply originated from snow melting on the surrounding mountain peaks, the estancia was likely one of the few locations on our globe where relatively pure untreated unpolluted drinking water was still available.

La Christina was located in a valley surrounded by an Antarctic climate, but the mountains reflected and concentrated the sun's rays to produce an oasis where Jean was able to cultivate a sizable vegetable garden and a flower garden containing mainly giant multi-coloured lupines. My visit in December 18-31, took place during Patagonia's summer.

Chatting with Jean, I asked, "Exactly how large is the estancia?" With a casual wave of her hand, she said, "It goes to those two mountains over there." Turning through 360 degrees, with another wave she continued, "And to those mountains over there."

After a two hour stroll, a hiker would find themselves alone, several miles from any other human beings on the planet. Although much of Patagonia was reminiscent of the bleak arid landscape of Siberia or Tibet, Jean's property contained a microcosm of small lakes and ponds which were home for ducks, geese, and a variety of other water fowl, and the vegetation in the valley and its features displayed almost every colour of the spectrum. I photographed one cascading mountain stream which exposed patterns in the rock strata, where the rich colours created a striking masterpiece which might have been painted by one of Canada's own Group of Seven artists. Mother Nature exhibited her sculpting powers as the stream scoured sandstone banks to the smoothness of velvet before disappearing into a bottomless vortex bored into the earth. From vantage points at the end of any walk, it was difficult to become lost, as the house with its surrounding poplars and evergreens stood out on the horizon as vividly as an island of vegetation in a sea of stone.

Jean's only concession to modern technology was a battery-operated radio used to order supplies or respond to an emergency. Jean's late husband Herbert had been an avid ham radio operator and his remaining antennae stood like the skeletons of prehistoric beasts overlooking the house. During his era at La Christina, Herbert Sr. had built a combination of wind and water generators to provide electricity to operate his radios and other electrical equipment. Besides a few rusty antennae, the only legacy remaining from Herbert's past, was one anemic wind generator which provided a dribble of electricity into its attached storage battery.

The property offered a wealth of photographic subjects, none of which were 'off-limits' during our visit. One day, I set out alone to explore the property, and after approximately thirty minutes, I realized that Jean's two German Shepherd pups had decided to tag along with me. I tried to get them to return to the house but had no success. Arriving at a fast flowing mountain stream, I thought this was an ideal spot to discourage my persistent little companions. I removed my hiking boots and socks and rolled my pant legs above my knees. The water temperature was ideal for polar bears, but all it did for me was to assure a rapid crossing of the stream. Glancing over my shoulder, I expected to see two pups making a hasty retreat back towards the house. Instead of a retreat, one pup was already half way across the stream behind me and his brother was launching himself from the shore and making a supreme effort to catch up. Not wishing to leave the pups on their own so far away from the house, I stretched out on my back on the bank and shared my lunch with them while they dried off and we all rested. Relaxing in the sun, I noticed several condors drifting in the air currents high overhead. I have the pups to thank for this enforced stop, as I realized, that the condors were endangered as was life on this estancia. To me the pups epitomized the determination of early Patagonia pioneer families like the Masters. When I arrived back at the house several hours later with the pups in tow and ready for another of Jean's delicious dinners, the smile on Jean's face made me realize how important the pups' return was to their mistress.

Aside from the many natural subjects on the estancia, there were two interesting architectural ones left over from the Masters sheep-ranching days. The first building was a rusty tin shed which had been used to shear sheep and then to store bales of fleece. This building presented an unlimited variety of rusty metal textures to photograph.

The second structure which intrigued me the most was a deserted bunkhouse. As a result of the depressed market, this building had not been used actively by gauchos and farm workers for almost half a century. Its interior which was muted by a generous layer of dust, contained, a jacket hanging on a rusty nail behind the door, a sheepskin draped over a dilapidated cot, spice canisters on a shelf above the dry sink in the kitchen, iron frying pans resting on tops of two black cast iron stoves and even a crumpled crossword puzzle lying on the floor of the outside privy. The dated newspapers adhering to the bunkhouse walls confirmed the number of years that the papers had held out the chilly mountain drafts.

I watched specks of dust settling through a patch of sunlight streaming through one of the cracked window panes, and felt as though I could expect to hear voices in the next room, or for exhausted workers to burst through the doorway in search of a spot to relax at the end of a long tough day of work. By all appearances, the occupants of the bunkhouse had left only recently, but all signs inside the building pointed to a life that existed in the 1940s. The ghostly bunkhouse stood as an era frozen in time. Based on my visit to the surroundings and my knowledge of Patagonia, the following paragraph describes an imaginary visit to the bunkhouse on a winter's day a half-century ago.

As I climbed the steps of the bunkhouse, an Antarctic gust transformed my breath into ice crystals, and snow crunched beneath my boots. Just inside the doorway, a row of heavy leather winter boots leaned against one another like an orchestra of exhausted concertinas. A collection of sheepskin coats, vests and woolen toques hung from pegs along one wall above the boots. All clothing placed the emphasis on function rather than style. The warmth inside the building was a welcome relief from the storm raging outside. My nostrils quivered from an array of smells ranging from sheep manure, to perspiration, stale wine, and pungent tobacco smoke. Some folks with sensitive nostrils might find these odours offensive, but to workers of the day, they were a comfortable blanket of familiarity. Most of these workers were swarthy half-breed Chilean Indians, many of whom wore black baggy war-surplus pants called bombachas. Several gauchos relaxed around a scarred wooden table as they slurped down sizeable goblets of vino Rosado.

In contrast to the earthy animal odours which smacked me in the face as I entered the doorway, from the cast iron wood stoves in the kitchen, mouth-watering aromas wafted out from a combination of bubbling pots of lamb stew, and several loaves of freshly baked bread which had just been removed from the oven.

The walls were papered creatively with old newspapers, some in English, but most in Spanish. Calendars, with photos of horses, landscapes, and even the image of a bare-breasted senorita, added variety to the ancient newspaper decor while un-papered areas were covered with large swathes of burlap salvaged from bales of fleece. In addition to being decorative, these wall coverings acted as insulation against the gusts of Antarctic breezes which sought to enter through unplugged cracks in the walls. On pleasant summer days, workers would spend their leisure hours outside, but at this time of year, they chose the interior which offered all of the comforts and familiarity of home.

Estancia Christina has had a colourful history as an operating sheep ranch, but it has also attracted a variety of adventure seeking visitors as well. In the mid-1900's, explorer Eric Shipton, and his party of three stopped in for a brief visit with the Masters. Shipton and his trio had been the first explorers to traverse the Patagonia Ice Cap. A team of Italian Mountain climbers also had used the estancia as a staging area while they made a series of attempts to climb mountain peaks nearby.

On Christmas morning of my visit, each member of our group received a token Christmas gift of a T-shirt from our travel company, but my greatest gift was the one I received from the two pups as they displayed such a sense of determination, and forced me to sit by the side of a mountain stream where I could watch circling condors overhead, and appreciate the beauty of that remote site.

On the final day of our visit, there was concern that our departure might be delayed due to high winds on Lago Argentino, but the winds subsided in time, the motor launch arrived, and we were able to return to Punta Bandera more or less on schedule. What had begun as a visit to an impossibly harsh landscape, turned out to be a revelation of how toughness, hospitality, and warmth of one elderly widow could overcome all of the ordeals that Patagonia, the Land of Big Feet could muster. Looking back on this experience a quarter of a century later, I doubt that the estancia still exists as it did at the time of our visit as investors had been tempting Jean to sell her property for an attractive price.

19 The Lure of the North

Having been born in the hamlet of Gold Centre in Northern Ontario, and after spending a month in Resolute Bay in 1961 interning with the RCAF after completing university, I was drawn north once again above the Arctic Circle to Resolute Bay in 1992. This last trip to the 'land of the midnight sun' was as a participant with Ecosummer Expeditions, as a member of the High Arctic Islands photographic expedition. For the August 8-20 trip I purchased 60 rolls of slide film at a cost of $603.75. This quantity of film allowed me the possibility of making 2,160 exposures.

A Canadian Airlines flight transported me from Toronto to Montreal then to Resolute Bay. While in Resolute, I toured the town where I visited an Inuit stone carver at work before our group departed via a twin-otter aircraft for the trip further north. During our visit to the Truelove Arctic Institute Base on Devon Island we bunked with scientists conducting research on Arctic flora and fauna. It was in the Truelove dining hall that I was asked to put my artistic talents to work. Trip organizers provided me with a can of black enamel and a brush which I used to paint the image of a walrus on the dining room wall, using a likeness obtained from material provided by Ecosummer Expeditions. My walrus stood, and I assume still stands, in

the Arctic beside work of Inuit artists depicting reindeer and other arctic wildlife. I chose to sign my masterpiece with the name 'Macoingatuk' which sounded to me like a good Inuit handle. It wasn't a work of art on quite the same scale as that of Michelangelo but it should perplex any viewers who might wonder at the identity of the artist who created that stunning walrus image.

While visiting Devon Island, I went tramping over the ice, snow and muskeg with my camera and spotted a small herd of muskoxen in the distance with a large boulder between me and the herd. I approached close enough to get a few long distance photos of animals that Inuit hunters referred to as 'Oomingmak' which translates as 'bearded one' in the Inuktatuk language. Muskoxen spend 4 months in darkness at temperatures of -30 and -40 degrees centigrade.Their coats consist of two layers, an under layer of fine wool of exceptional warmth and an outer layer of long shaggy hair hanging nearly to the ground. These layers of hair allow the animals to survive the bone-chilling arctic blizzards. As I approached the large boulder, a bull muskox was standing alone, perhaps curious about me, or possibly just intent on protecting the herd. The bull approached my rock from his side while with the aid of my long-distance lens I was able to obtain a full head shot of the animal's bloodshot eyes and curved horns. The magnificent bull chose not to investigate my side of the rock but instead wandered back to the herd.

To answer the call of nature at the Truelove base, the scientists used a privy which was located in an open space a short distance from the main buildings. Due to winds which were often gale force, the privy was anchored to the ground by several stout ropes. The bottom section of the outhouse contained a metal barrel into which waste dropped for disposal later. In my fertile imagination I visualized the privy breaking loose from its moorings, and being carried aloft by gale force winds. I imagined the impact of the airborne outhouse striking the ground again with its load of poop. This would surely create quite a splash on the arctic landscape.

Since the small outhouse was located in an open space away from the other structures, one might wonder if it was occupied. To answer that question, a chunk of wooden dowling with a flag attached hung just inside the privy's door. While 'doing one's business,' the dowling with its attached flag was left clearly visible outside indicating the facility was in use. When they left, the occupant would remove the flag and place it inside for the next visitor. This could leave anyone wishing to use the toilet in an uncomfortable position if the previous occupant forgot to take down the flag when leaving.

Our accommodation in the arctic consisted most often of an insulated free-standing bell tent resting on the snow covered terrain, with mattresses on which to place sleeping bags. At one location scientists had constructed a fibreglass sauna shaped like an igloo since showers weren't available. The routine after taking a sauna was to roll in the snow. On Ellesmere Island, on a trip by inflatable zodiac, our group set out to view and photograph a walrus family on an ice flow. There was always the risk in such cases that an enraged bull walrus might attack the zodiac and sink its tusks into the inflatable craft. The walrus family that we approached seemed not to be bothered by our approach however, so I managed to obtain several photos of the family. One photo showed an agile female leaning backwards resting on one flipper as if she was break-dancing. We also had time on this island to visit an RCMP post which at the time was no longer in use. White painted rocks lined a path leading to and joining the two police buildings. At this stop we had time to visit Twin Glacier Valley where we could actually walk inside the glacier and view the fantastic blue and green hues of the ice pack. When we left

Ellesmere our twin-otter aircraft on the way back to Resolute landed on Beechey Island where Franklin's ships overwintered in the 1800's. A memorial on the beach marked the gravesite of crew member John Torrington who died along with Franklin. Following our arrival back in Resolute, our arctic expedition came to an end and we headed back to civilization via Baffin Island, Montreal, Toronto and finally Orangeville.

20 A Chip Off The Old Block

I have documented many of my assorted hobbies previously in this memoir but have said little about my woodcarving activities. The following story is representative of that part of my life:

Rottweilers Indians and eagles were challenges in my latest woodcarving project.

When Kim, my Cherokee niece asked me to consider doing a woodcarving, I agreed on the understanding that since she had no preference as to subject, the choice would be mine. In deference to her native heritage and my interest in human faces and eagles, I settled on carving a North American Indian bust wearing an eagle's head war bonnet. For the piece, I selected a section of a maple trunk measuring to approximately my chest height, and of sufficient diameter to accommodate a life size human head.

I retrieved a set of my carving books in storage with the Silver Headed Woodpeckers carving club at the Orangeville Seniors' Centre, then began by drawing a rough paper pattern of my idea. Proportions were key for both the native and eagle heads. The relationship between width, height, and depth of the heads are critical to produce realistic features. I used callipers and dividers to transfer my pattern's measurements roughly onto the maple block, and a small electric chainsaw was instrumental to rough out the complete piece. The original section of maple weighed almost as much as I did, but by the time the work was roughed out, I could manhandle the piece using a dolly to transport the work into my nephew Shawn's shop in case of inclement weather. When possible, I preferred to work outside, fanned by gentle breezes, with leaves fluttering down around me, and the sun shining.

Rottweilers Lily and Ben were my companions during much of my working time. An unexpected complication at the beginning of each carving session was to pacify friendly leaping mutts with lapping tongues. Since my work area was located within the dogs' fenced in living space, I scanned the area and cleaned up any of the dogs' calling cards into which I might inadvertently tread. Ben once attempted to use my carving as his own personal fire hydrant, but Kim quickly squelched that idea.

My preferred tools for carving were chisels and mallet, but a chainsaw, Dremel and angle grinder were concessions to electrical tools for rough cuts and finer details. During the actual carving process, I always erred on the side of excess. I would construct a feature, such as a nose, larger than intended, in case I had to move its position slightly or alter its size as I worked towards the final result. There is always the unexpected in natural material such as wood. A carver might encounter rot or imperfections in growth or grain of the selected material. In my case, I rooted out a number of small white grubs which had taken up residence and were likely the culprits which caused the original maple's demise.

When the carving was nearly complete and I was almost ready to consider a final stain and wood finish, I left the piece outside for several days on the shop's porch. A woodpecker took that opportunity to attack my masterpiece, perhaps wishing to help me complete my work, but more likely it was searching for more white grubs that might still have been lodged in the wood. The indentations which the bird made on the carving were not catastrophic, but did force me to incorporate its efforts into my work before I could consider the piece suitable for application of the final finish.

Following the completion of my project, I have renewed

respect for the carvings scattered about the town of Orangeville. In my opinion, these works of art are awelcome addition to the uniqueness of the town. Instead of, simply chopping down and disposing of dead maples, what better way to document Orangeville's rustic heritage? I know that the artists who completed the town's wood sculptors faced many of the same design and structural problems that I did but hopefully, their main critics are citizens of the town rather than Rottweilers and woodpeckers.

With my memoir rolling along, I'd like to tie up a few loose ends, summarize my life, and make a few observations of what I've learned about myself while offering a few words of advice as to how I've managed to pursue a life well lived.

I consider myself fortunate having been born into a family with such firstrate parents. Being the youngest of seven kids, five boys and two girls, I wouldn't actually call our family a loving relationship. We had our squabbles such as when I fought with my sister Ruby who chased me down when it came time to fulfill my designated job of helping her dry the dishes, but in general we got along with each other and were always around when needed (and still are). When my father died in 1986 in his 89th year, I began a practice that I've continued to this day. At the visitation for father at the funeral home, the minister who would be conducting the service asked my brother Gerry, "What kind of man was your father?" Gerry replied, and rightly so, "He had been in the army, he worked on the railroad, and he worked in the McIntyre Gold Mine."

To me, these occupations did not sum up father's true character. Shortly after that conversation, I sought out the minister and spent three-quarters of an hour, bending his ear, telling him about father's habits, and what made father in my eyes the great man that he was. Happily the minister used many of my comments in the final service summarizing father as, "The salt of the earth, a man who was a general practitioner in life but a specialist in the art of living." Brother Vance who was probably the least well educated of the kids in the family expressed the feelings of the rest of us when last viewing father lying in an open coffin. He bent down and kissed him on the lips. All that I could manage was to touch father's lifeless hand, but I expressed my appreciation of dad in words to the minister who was then able to incorporate my thoughts of appreciation into words at the final service.

When mother died in 1996 at the age of 96, I had written a brief family history which contained many references to mother and father, much of which was presented in a humorous vein. I presented my written work to the minister who was to conduct mother's final service. The reverend asked for my permission to allow him to use my writing in connection with his eulogy. I readily allowed the minister to use my stories and believe that the rest of the family appreciated my words of affection. My stories reflected their feelings and gave the service more of a human touch with an air of levity that I'm sure mother would have appreciated. As a result of my writing, the minister described father as 'the salt of the earth', while mother was the 'pepper' which infused their relationship. (An excellent analogy.) Since the passing of my parents, I also supplied a eulogy at a service for my sister Ruby when her life ended as a result of cancer.

21 Two Thousand Pounds
of Bacon and Bone

During the 1960's, I continued my education at Queen's University in Kingston before embarking on a teaching career, a factor which kept me occupied for the next thirty-four years. It was while I was at university that Mother's brother Howard Hurley was most active in pursuing his pastime of training Rusty & Red, a team of Tamworth hogs which Howard groomed to pull a wagon which he christened the Hurleyville Taxi. During my life, I was so taken with Howard's achievement, when I retired and had the time, I hoped to publish Howard's story after I'd learned more details of his accomplishments. I wished my account to be factually correct, but didn't want to write a book simply of facts. My objective was to compose a humorous account which any reader would enjoy.

When I retired from teaching in 1995, I had time to research as many details as I could so that I could do justice to Howard's story and record it for posterity. In order to hone my writing skills with the objective of recounting the Hurleyville Taxi story, I enrolled in a correspondence writing course, 'Breaking Into Print' as offered by LongRidge Writers Group in Connecticut. I knew very little about the publishing business at the time but my intention was to self-publish the book after I had completed writing the story.

My first line of attack in researching Howard's story was to meet with Howard's son Ross in Echo Bay. From information gleaned during my conversation with Ross, I learned more about Howard's methods and itinerary as he displayed his team of trained hogs around the Ontario and Western Canada. Ross provided me with a good deal of information including the loan of a set of books containing lists of names of visitors who had ridden in the 'Taxi.' The ledgers also contained writings by Howard in the form of a personal diary. My travels in search of Howard's past stemmed from a particular name and phone contained within the ledgers I'd borrowed from Ross Hurley. During Howard's road trips with the Hurleyville Taxi, he ventured out to Western Canada where he was invited to attend the Threshermens' Reunion. It was during this trip that Howard met Russ Gurr, a professional musician known as 'the Singing Farmer.' I learned that Russ still lived in Brandon, Manitoba and I discovered that his phone number had not changed from that contained in the ledgers I had borrowed from Ross.

As a result of my phone call to Brandon, I arranged to drive west and meet with Russ from whom I hoped to gain more information about Howard and the team's western tour. Although Russ was in his 80's, he chauffeured me around Brandon in his pickup while we chatted, and after my visit which lasted a week, Russ provided me with tapes of his songs and granted me permission to use his songs written about the Hurleyville Taxi to promote the sale of my book once it was published. Although my trip to Brandon took place in October, I ran into blizzard conditions on the return leg of my journey. This made my driving back a major challenge, but the trip was well worth what I gained.

Russ died soon after my book was published but not before I sent him a copy. Via the internet I discovered a couple who raised Tamworths near Trenton. I paid them a visit to supplement my knowledge of Howard's pigs, and as a result of that visit, a story appeared in the Sault Star about my intention to publish a book. Richard Mousseau, owner of Moose Hide Press contacted me with an offer to publish my story. I accepted his offer then set out to travel to gain as much information as I could to complete the story. I provided pen & ink illustrations and in 2001, the book was published. Nancy Frater of BookLore in Orangeville arranged a book launch and the Orangeville Banner newspaper provided excellent coverage. I had a great turn out, so guess that I can now call myself an author. It is sad that mother could not have been alive to see the finished book,

but I dedicated it in her memory. She would have been proud, but more importantly she would have been able to supply a wealth of family background material and perhaps might have revealed a few family skeletons which Howard might have just as soon be left in the closet.

Ripley's—Believe It or Not!

TEAM OF BOARS
TRAINED TO PULL A WAGON IN HARNESS
OWNED BY HOWARD HURLEY, Echo Bay, Ont.

22 A River Runs Through It

In 1992 I purchased a copy of the book, *A River Runs Through It*, by Norman Maclean and also viewed the movie by the same name. This was my first exposure to the concept of fly fishing. The movie bordered on the spiritual at times. Fly casting and watching the line dancing from the reel appeared to me much like calligraphy. Inspired by both the book and movie, I purchased my own fly fishing rod along with several books on fly casting techniques. Not being one to take on an activity by half measures, I also participated in a fly tying workshop so that I could create my own unique flies. Squirreled away in my belongings, I still own a vice for use in tying flies, and my box of hooks and related paraphernalia also contains a variety of coloured feathers and furs for use tying some of my own original creations.

I once visited a stocked trout pond north of Orangeville where I tried my hand at casting and even managed to hook one small trout. Although I have never gone on a fly fishing expedition with fishermen who were skilled in the art, doing so is one of the items I'd still like to accomplish. Considering the speed with which the environment is unravelling, the likelihood of finding a choice fishing river is becoming slimmer as time passes.

As I have been working on this memoir, I have been seeking an answer to the question, "is there a golden thread that runs through my life connecting the many activities in which I have been involved?" If one considers life to be a river, perhaps I have been casting my line of curiosity out seeking answers to many questions which I keep encountering. The number of instances when fishing has appeared in this memoir is making me wonder if that isn't the spiritual representation of the golden thread for which I've been searching.

When I joined the Headwaters Writer Guild in Orangeville around 2008, Len Rich was a member of that writing group. It wasn't until later that I discovered that Len besides being a writer was also an accomplished fly fisherman. Len operated his own fishing lodge in Eastern Canada and at one time he earned the Governor General's award for his work related to the environment. From a writing perspective as well, Len has written a newspaper column featuring characters and stories which reflect my own tastes. At the time I joined the group, Len and I constituted most of the male portion of an Orangeville writing group dominated by females.

When Len was diagnosed with cancer and was fighting the disease back in 2009, I sent the following note to him hoping to lift his spirits.

Dear Len,

Here are a few thoughts for you to ponder. In the words of author conservationist and philosopher Henry David Thoreau: **"Many men go fishing all of their lives without knowing it is not fish they are after."**

I don't think that you are one of those men. Unfortunately our paths did not cross until relatively late in our lives. It was not until I read your book 'Memoirs of a Fly Fisher' that I realized how passionate you are about fishing. I own a fly fishing rod, and have tried my hand at tying flies, but I consider myself to be a 'closet' fly fisherman, with very little practical experience in the sport.

I'm not sure what attracted you to fly fishing, but for me, I view a fly line dancing through the air as being almost a form of calligraphy. There is no doubt in my mind that fly fishing and watching a fly cast is an art form

I don't know whether or not you are a religious man, but in Norman Maclean's book, "A River Runs Through It." Maclean starts off by saying, "there is no clear line between religion and fly fishing."

In your memoir, you mention, "The placid stillness of a remote stream, feeling the pull of current against your legs, casting methodically to a place where you feel your quarry might be lying in wait, the thrill of a fish rising to your offering, and finally feeling the weight of the fish at the end of your wispy rod." This suggests to me that for you, fly fishing can be a very spiritual experience.

Later you go on to say. "I think all of us dream one day of finding a place somewhere in the world where streams run cold and clear, wild life cavorts freely, waters teem with battling fish, the surrounding landscape is breathtaking, and Nature has not been ruined by the onslaught of man.

Just after a blazing sunset, a full moon rose on the horizon and bathed us in a cool white glow. I'll never forget the first time I saw the lake. It lay like a glistening emerald nestled beneath the sweeping green hills of spruce and fir, dwarfed by a panorama of distant mountains which still contained patches of snow from the previous winter.

Perhaps it is the urge in all of us to enjoy at least once in a lifetime, a special experience in a special place where time has been suspended and you can still feel as one with Nature, this experience, that's what I've found at Awesome Lake, is my idea of what Heaven should be like to anyone who understands the pleasure of fly fishing."

I don't consider myself to be one of the fortunate ones in your cadre of fly fishing friends, so I'll limit my remarks to the other interest that we have in common. I think that you are one of the fortunate men who has been able to immerse yourself in two loves of your life; those of fly fishing and writing. You have readily shared your writing secrets, enthusiasm, and encouragement with other writers, just as you did your fishing secrets, with anyone who cared to listen. You might not realize it, but I believe you treated your writing in the same enthusiastic way that you treated a fly fishing excursion.

At a meeting of the Headwaters Writer Guild, you would settle comfortably into your chair immersing yourself chest deep in the meeting, waiting expectantly for the first writing prompt to be given and you quivered with enthusiasm as you worked on that meeting's prompt. We could always expect you to have a unique angle to the particular prompt that was assigned.

Many of your friends are familiar with you for your fly fishing expertise, writings on fly tying, fishing trips, and conservation, but I particularly enjoyed your writing about ordinary folks such as the ones who populated your Back East newspaper column; the likes of Herb, Amanda, Martha, Oscar, and Carmine, and their zany antics. Your stories, "A Christmas Without Charlie," and "Tales of Christmas," in the anthology are great examples of pathos. I have to admit however that your account of the lawyer who dropped his false teeth through the seat of the fishing camp's outdoor privy, then attempted to use his fishing expertise to retrieve the lost dentures will always be at the top of my list of unforgettable fishing stories.

Many folks in this life create nary a ripple, but your full life as a recognized fisherman, conservationist and writer, have been proudly recorded for everyone to see. I feel fortunate to have had the opportunity to have shared chats and writing experiences with you. The members of our writing group miss your colourful writing, ready wit, encouragement, and professionalism, but most of all, I miss another friendly male face in the Headwaters Writers Guild, a group dominated by a bevy of lively ladies. (Or is it boisterous broads?) I'll let you decide which term is most appropriate. We did have two new male members appear at our last meeting. They both read some of their own high quality work which we all enjoyed, so I hope they will both persist and continue with the group. Our thoughts will be with you during your recovery. I'm sure that a good dose of creative writing will give you a good boost to get you back on your feet quicker! All the best!!!

Clare McCarthy

I was pleased to hear from Len's partner, Sue, that Len was very touched by my letter. Sadly, Len lost his fight with cancer, so I was glad that I had expressed my feelings towards him rather than wait until it was too late.

I attended a memorial service for Len Rich at the local trout fishing club. When speakers had presented all of the accolades, I ended the words of praise by reading one of Len's own stories about the Philadelphia lawyer visiting Len's fishing camp. Len's story described how the lawyer accidentally coughed up his dentures after a night of boozing. The set of teeth fell down through the hole of an outside privy and the lawyer attempted to retrieve his lost choppers using his rod and reel. Those in attendance at Len's memorial service thanked me for telling Len's story in his own words. This story echoed Len's sense of humour and displayed his great writing skills.

Visiting an Old Vet

I spent several years visiting Jim Wilson, a Second World War vet in a retirement home in Beeton. Jim had spent five years incarcerated in a German prisoner of war camp. He shared his experiences with me, and I put together for Jim several copies of his own biography, complete with photos. At the service following Jim's death, I shared with those present a few of the humorous events in Jim's life. I must admit that I was overly verbose in telling Jim's stories. It looks as though my lot in life is too make sure that any of my deceased friends aren't allowed to leave this earthly pale without the real stories of their lives being told with a touch of levity.

23 More Philosophical Ponderings

My wife Dorothy and I have remained wed for fifty years (and counting) and there are those who would ask what our secret is to a lengthy wedded life. Dorothy would probably say, "It's better to stay with the Devil you know rather than the one you don't!" I on the other hand would say that it's likely due to both of us having a sense of humour. When she asked me after one disagreement, "Why don't you ever argue?" My reply, "Why argue when I'm right?" went over like a lead balloon, and did little to improve that testy situation. When I spent time in Sunnybrook after getting smacked by a car, Dorothy played the part of Florence Nightingale incessantly hovering around my bedside.

When she had a triple bypass and later fractured her pelvis, it was I who donned Florence Nightingale's trappings, looking after her and taking on household jobs which Dorothy usually completed. So I suppose we have always been there for each other in times of stress. We talk a lot with each other, sharing our thoughts, which leads to fewer surprises or misunderstandings. Dorothy does not envy me indulging in some of my hair-brained schemes alone, antics such as a trip to the Amazon Jungle, sleeping with cockroaches or snoozing in a tent on the ice in the Canadian Arctic, or any other such cockymammy suggestion that I might come up with. On the other hand, we have shared some civilized travel adventures together to places such as Britain by used car, Ireland from one bed & breakfast to another, then by Irish busses. A trip to New Orleans by car, to Moosenee by train, then camper to Key West Florida, a flight to Wales and we shared a belated honeymoon in the Seychelles, one thousand miles in the Indian ocean off the coast of Africa thus rounding out our togetherness. (The Seychelles are islands in the sun with bed & breakfast establishments, and for me, topless beaches and plenty of walking.) We even visited the Alaska Highway by camper and the fog bound islands of Ste.Pierre & Miquelon. I have traveled to Newfoundland once alone with my Border Collie Mirk and four times with Dorothy. (Dorothy and I have another visit pending in 2015.)

Our daughter Margaret Anne was born in 1969 and presently lives in her own townhouse in Orangeville. She lives not far from us and we seldom see her (unless she wants something) but I know that if we needed her she would not hesitate to supply assistance, and advice (whether we needed it or not). All I have to do is look at Margaret Anne to realize the influence of genetics. As long as Margaret is around, my late mother will never be far away. The resemblance to Margaret's grandmother is so amazing.

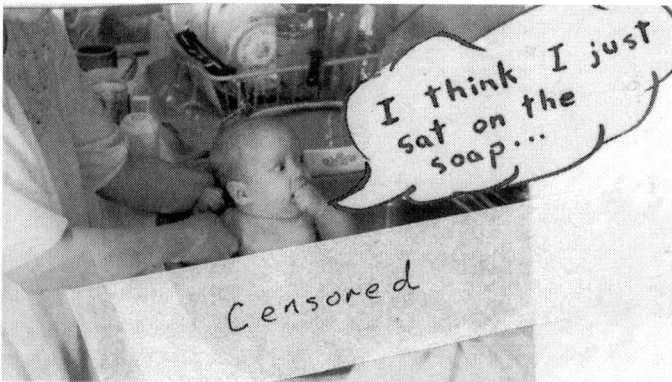

Margaret is single, with no expectations (that we know of) of getting married, but that part of her life is completely up to her. Better to be happy single, than miserable married (I won't say "like me", or I'd never hear the end of it).

If I look upon life as being a long winding river rather than a placid pond, my bicycle accident could be considered to be a turbulent set of rapids with which I had to contend. I'm not proud of everything that I've done in life. One of the little ripples was my stint as a budding kleptomaniac. During my early teen years, we did our share of shoplifting. We pilfered items such as toys and other small items that I considered essential but couldn't afford. There was no excuse for such behaviour, and I know my parents would be embarrassed to learn of such goings on. In Mother's words, I'd probably be "Skinned alive" or at the very least, "Have my hide tanned!" Another aspect of that time in my life was likely due to over-active hormones. I shared with some of my friends, nudist Nature magazines containing photos of buxom bare beauties playing volleyball, among other activities. Nature magazines were the only erotic literature available, as 'glossies' such as Playboy and Penthouse were not yet then available on the newsstands.

One of the loose ends which needs gathering relates to living accommodations. When Dorothy and I came to Orangeville in 1965, there were few apartments available in town. To provide a roof over our heads we purchased an old red brick farm house in town for the princely sum of $14,000. This old structure was always known as 'the Old Bully House' even after we took it over. Along with the house, we inherited a family of bats which at night would swoop out from under the eaves returning before dawn. House flies had become a problem in the spring when they would appear buzzing in the sunlight of a window. Following principal Maurice Cline's advice to

be my own self-exterminator, I sprayed the attic with insecticide and when I did so, it drove the bugged insects down into the lower rooms requiring us to vacuum up the dead bodies off the floor.

I constructed our own personal sauna in the garage attached to the house, and used a tank of propane from a BBQ and an old heater from a hot water tank as the rock heating source. We invited fellow teachers over for a sauna, after which the group retired to the back yard for a hose down with cold water. Our screams at such times probably made neighbours wonder what was happening to the tranquility of their neighbourhood.

To help cover our mortgage expenses, I added kitchen cupboards to one room of the 'Old Bully' house allowing us to rent part of the house as an apartment. But when the couple renting the apartment purchased a piano, and we had to listen to their serenades, we terminated the rental agreement. A real estate agent who later advertised the house for sale listed my addition as a 'butler's pantry' a ludicrous stretch of the imagination. The house had two sets of stairs to the upper floor. One front set with a banister near the main entrance of the house and a smaller set up through the kitchen The house still stands to date (but probably without the bats) but its price has escalated to the hundreds of thousands of dollars.

Following the sale of 'bat hall' we purchased a new two-story house in which I used beams rescued from a barn in Shelburne and limestone from the barn's foundation to renovate the basement to resemble an English pub. I created a fireplace equipped with a heat producing insert and we hired a professional to construct a brick chimney outside the house. A poor footing on his part, resulted in the chimney leaning like the notorious tower of Pizza.

I have three vices to which I must confess. The first is hats. My mother informed me, that as a little kid, I used to stand in front of our mirror admiring myself wearing a hat. To that end, over the years I have owned enough hats to equip every resident of China. I have ball caps, berets, toques, two green Irish Derbys, multi-Tilley hats, panama hats and even one from the Seychelles made from banana leaves.

My second vice is buying books, mostly new, but often ones that are used or out of print. My backlog of unread books should keep me going until eternity, but I still keep buying more. How nuts can any person be? Since Dorothy and I are health conscious, we must have copies of every diet book that's ever been written.

My third vice is being a pack rat. (Are there more vices I've overlooked?) I hate to throw anything away, so tend to hoard stuff that any normal person would have thrown away years ago. This makes being untidy inevitable. Being health conscious, both Dorothy and I attempt to eat meals that are as nourishing as possible. Unfortunately Dorothy is an excellent cook and enjoys cooking, and I enjoy eating. Consequently, her prepared desserts are my weakness. To combat the accumulation of increased poundage, I walk a lot, belong to a local gym, and have recently purchased a Tread Climber, a pricey contraption which I have been putting to good use since I purchased it. I have no intention of letting the machine gather dust, but I'm sure that some folks would consider me crazy to waste cash on such nonsense. Dorothy often says, "You'll be the healthiest corpse in the cemetery!" Since my age is presently three-quarters of a century and my aim is to live for a full century, I need all the help I can get.

Some people might say that I put my foot in my mouth too often, but I like to think that I live by the philosophy of the late Pete Seeger. The following story is a reflection of my beliefs and those of the famous activist musician.

To Everything There Is A Season

To everything there is a season, and a time to every purpose under heaven: A time to be born, and a time to die. (Book of Ecclesiastes 3, Verses 1-8)

May 1969 was a time that Dorothy and I attended a performance by Peter Seeger at Massey Hall theatre in Toronto while January 27, 2014 was the time that Peter Seeger died at the age of ninety-four. Active and robust to the end, he was chopping wood ten days prior to his death.

I have just finished listening to a unique cassette tape which I made of Seeger's live 1969 show in Toronto. Since audio tapes have a limited life, I recently had it transferred to a CD to ensure the recording's longevity. It was great listening to the performance again, hearing Pete chatting with his audience and encouraging them to sing along while at the same time urging everyone to support the grape boycott in California.

Pete Seeger was musician, songwriter, activist and accomplished player of banjo, guitar, recorder, tin whistle, mandolin, piano and ukulele; but it was his command of the 5-string banjo that particularly caught my fancy. Over the years, I have owned several inexpensive 5-string banjos, none of which I ever mastered. In spite of that, approximately two years ago, I shelled out enough cash to purchase a good quality Goodtime five-string banjo. I think the time has come to disprove the hoary saying, "You can't teach an old dog, new tricks." I'm sure my banjo playing will never produce another Pete Seeger, but I feel it's always good to have a challenge in life. Surely, even the non-musically inclined can learn to play an instrument late in life. We can all learn from stands that Pete Seeger has taken, the following quotations being examples of his advice:

"Education is when you read the fine print.

Experience is what you get if you don't.

It is very important to learn to talk to people

you disagree with.

If there's something wrong, speak up!

Songs won't save the planet

but neither will books or speeches.

Technology will save us, if it doesn't wipe us out first"

Some of his well-known hits include, *"To Everything there is a Season, If I Had a Hammer, Where Have All the Flowers Gone? Goodnight Irene, So Long Its Been Good To Know You* and *We Will Overcome."* Pete Seeger was hailed by some folks as America's conscience, and he was an a example of a man who knew the difference between living life peacefully and going through it quietly. On the body of his banjo appeared the message, "This machine surrounds hate and forces it to surrender."

Canada has produced its own brand of legendary entertainer in the person of Stompin' Tom Connors. Tom died too early at the age of seventy-seven in 2013. Tom Connors was not a protestor in quite the same sense as Pete Seeger, but he was outspoken when it came to recognizing old folks and promoting Canadian values. Stompin' Tom Connors was proud to call himself a Canadian, and his songs were based on Canadians and their eccentricities. Tom's values and priorities should be apparent from his following thoughts, "I began to hear a lot more stories being told by the old-timers, I could see that life in the community had been a lot more interesting in their day than it was now. For one thing, I could see that each of them was an individual character unto himself. Each had a rich history of doing things in his own way. Each seemed to have an independent, undying spirit. And each seemed to have that special something that I was looking for." It was around such characters that Tom Connors wove his songs about: *Big Joe Mufferaw of Ottawa, Bingo on A Sudbury Saturday Night, The Tobacco fields of Tillsonburg, Bud The Spud and The Hockey Song.*

Even Canadian environmentalist David Suzuki realized the importance of music. "As a geneticist I'm fascinated by the built-in need we have for music; it reaches deep within us. The power of a good song to touch us emotionally and rally us to action is nothing short of extraordinary."

Have there ever been two more colourful entertainers than Pete Seeger and Stompin' Tom Connors? If they had appeared on the stage together, I'm sure they would have rocked the music world with their raucous tunes. As it is, they have both made contributions to the conscience of the world by stands that they took on world peace, the environment, human rights and standing up for what they believed in. Their performances individually were entertaining, but if more people took a page from the books on their philosophies of life, the world would be a much better place.

I would suggest that you follow Pete Seeger's advice: "If there's something wrong, speak up!" Also, I'd like to think of myself as a man like Seeger who knows the difference between living a life peacefully and going through it quietly. I'll never be another Pete Seeger, but he certainly possessed traits to which it is worth aspiring. I hope to gain some facility with the five-string banjo, but certainly not to the level of Seeger. I don't plan to attend demonstrations as he did, but I made my voice heard through editorial cartoons and any published writing whenever I could.

24 Leaner and Meaner

Our recent purchase of a new dining room suite appears to have launched me into a leaner and meaner phase of my life. When Dorothy recommended making the purchase of dining room furniture so that she could better display her Belleek china and other cherished crockery, I didn't realize that this would present two problems. First, the contents of the ten boxes containing the table and chairs that arrived, had to be put together. Who better to ask for assistance than my octogenarian brother Eldon? He had worked in the 1950's on the assembly of the Avro Arrow supersonic fighter aircraft. Following his instructions, assembling the dining room suite should thus be a breeze! I emptied the boxes keeping the contents of each together to avoid confusion, then we began. Eldon parked himself comfortably on a chair, "That bolt goes in that hole, put on two washers, then a nut, snug it up, but not too tight."

After we had finished assembling the first four chairs, numbers five and six had arms so we altered our routine to accommodate them. When the time came to assemble the table, I emptied the respective boxes, but there were no assembly instructions for the table in sight, not even a picture of the completed item! My heart skipped a few beats at the thought of our dilemma. Dorothy informed us that the table didn't have four legs but rather two pedestals with supporting smaller legs. Eldon didn't seem to be perturbed, "Let's see what we've got. Those must be the pedestals. These pieces must be the supports. That bolt goes in there. Put washers and a nut on."

Following his logic, we discussed the possibilities deciding that a plate could be attached to the top of each pedestal and by lining up bolt holes we could bolt each pedestal to the table top. In the end, everything went together nicely. Fortunately the china cabinet came assembled and all that was required was to install three glass shelves. The table hasn't collapsed yet, nor have the six chairs, so I guess having the advice from a big brother can help overcome what appears to be a challenging dilemma.

The new purchase created a second problem. "What do we do with the old dining room suite?" We planned to give it away, but to whom? I made two contacts in Orangeville, but they both fell through so I telephoned our friends, the Hinnells in Hamilton to enquire about listing it on the internet. Several minutes after my phone call with Jackie in Hamilton, she called back and asked, "Can we have the old dining room suite?" She wanted to put it in a garage sale that their church was having in April, so I agreed, with the proviso, "All you have to do is pick it up!" We arranged a date, and they arrived with a trailer which we loaded, then treated them to a Swiss Chalet lunch and our old dining room suite disposal problem was solved!

The Hamilton church garage sale inspired Dorothy and I to take a meaner-leaner look at our accumulated collectables that we seldom used. We now have a living room strewn with boxes, and will be glad to get rid of a lot of little-used stuff which in the process will go towards God's work. I recently bought a new Bose audio system, so can now recycle the old sound system off to Hamilton as well.

In hopes of gaining a leaner physique, I succumbed to ads on TV to purchase that previously mentioned exercise machine called a Bowflex TreadClimber. I nearly had to mortgage the house to purchase it, but though it was worth the cost. When the four boxes arrived, one weighed in excess of 200 pounds, but I managed to wrestle the four cartons to the basement for unpacking.

The assembly manual for the contraption surfaced in the bottom of the biggest box. Looking over the fifteen assembly steps, one stood out. **"Note: Do Not Cut The Shipping Zip-Tie Until Instructed!"** By then I'd already cut said zip-tie, so once again I called on Eldon to help assemble this more challenging project. We followed the assembly steps and proceeded as before with the dining room suite and after two days had a complete functioning TreadClimber. The inadvertently cut zip-tie made our work a little more complicated, but we managed. The only mishap occurred when I inadvertently dropped one of the weighty pieces onto Eldon's hand. It took off a chunk of his hide and out came the band aids to staunch the flow of blood. In light of the bandages necessary to patch Eldon's hand, his daughter-in-law Kim made the request. "You tell Uncle Clare not to buy anything in the future that will require your help to put it together!"

I've been using the Bowflex daily for the past three months and fully expect to have improved weight loss, improved conditioning, improved blood pressure readings and a physique that will soon resemble that of a Greyhound rather than a walrus. I attribute my recent successful physical exam by Dr. Josephson as being in part due to my recently purchased TreadClimber but also continued healthy eating.

Since I have been a packrat, I also hope to become meaner and leaner by overcoming my long ingrained habit of hoarding and will try to reduce my treasure trove of junk that I seldom use any more. More recently, my TreadClimber use has tapered off somewhat, but not to zero. Eating less seems to be more effective than exercise to lose weight.

25 Crazy as an Outhouse Rat

During the last few years of my teaching career, I frequently used the phrase, 'Crazy as an outhouse rat' to describe my colleagues who acted strangely. Perhaps anyone who has read this memoir would be correct in inferring that the 'crazy' phrase described me as well as my colleagues. Three cases come to mind to substantiate a belief that I might have more than one 'screw loose.'

Several years ago, my wife and I, along with Gus and Jan Dickson visited the Harbour Castle Hilton Hotel in Toronto. After enjoying a meal in the hotel's revolving tower dining room, Dorothy and I retired to the basement to investigate the hotel's gift shop. It must have been early October, because a latex mask for sale caught my attention. The mask was a caricaturist impression of Quebec separatist, Rene Levesque with a cigarette dangling from his lower lip. Since Rene usually wore a trench coat, and I was wearing one at the time, I paid for the mask, then slipped it over my head. With my hands in my pockets, I then sauntered through the hotel lobby chuckling softly, "heh, heh,heh" in typical Rene Levesque fashion. As I meandered through the hotel lobby and past the hotel's desk the young lady on duty was understandably surprised at my appearance. In hindsight, I consider myself lucky that she did not alert armed hotel security to warn them that a dangerous lunatic was on the loose. Why I did what I did at that time is a complete mystery to me. It just seemed like the obvious thing to do.

A Halloween mask gambit came to the fore once again several years later. This time it was a latex depiction of Albert Einstein with frizzy hair, bushy moustache and bulbous nose. With the mask fitting entirely over my head I decided to wear it around Halloween to a department heads meeting at Orangeville High School where I worked at the time. Since Principal Jack McFadden had a sense of humour, I showed up early for the meeting wearing the mask. As others arrived I sat at the table and watched the mixed reactions of fellow department heads as they entered the room. I did eventually remove the mask when it was time to begin the scheduled business. Some of my colleagues at the time thought that me wearing the mask was a definite improvement on my features.

The third mask incident occurred in Orillia. I was visiting friend Len Johnson at the Mezza Luna Cafe. While Len sipped on his coffee, I got up and retired to the washroom, where I slipped on the Einstein mask. When I returned and sat down in my recently vacated seat, I expected that Len would immediately realize it was me. Len's reaction however was at first one of fright. Luckily, I'm not rueing the day that I acted like a jackass causing him a case of cardiac failure.

26 Sausages & Eggs Over Easy and the French Connection

One of the difficulties in writing a memoir such as this, is to know which facts to include, and which to omit. I have probably inadvertently omitted some events due to memory loss on my part so I have presented a draft copy of this memoir to Len Johnson, asking for suggestions from Len and his wife Mary. Len and I have spent many hours in Orillia over coffee and breakfast chatting and chuckling about our Irish relatives. Len is an ex-Roman Catholic priest, poet, storyteller, conscientious objector, and a man who participates in many activities in his home town and environs. I respect Len's judgement, and I asked him to look over this memoir and offer any comments which he felt were relevant. Even after my Einstein mask caper, Len didn't have second thoughts about agreeing to my request but I found him reserved in his comments, not wishing to put words in my mouth.

Over a recent breakfast at Hill's Restaurant in Orillia, Len offered two comments about my memoir. First, he thought that along with other adjectives I'd used to describe my personality, I should include the word versatile. Len also felt that towards the end of the memoir my travel writing was a bit 'thin,' a term upon which he did not elaborate.

Since Len Johnson admires the writing of Irish author James Joyce (as do I) Len made some interesting observations about the draft copy of my memoir. My typing was not without several errors in spelling and grammar. Len ordered me to retain two of the spelling mistakes which he referred to as "Joycean mistakes." Len felt that retaining these errors which were similar to those purposeful mistakes incorporated in Joyce's own writing would provide an interesting dimension to my memoir. How could I not follow Len's advice to follow a technique espoused by James Joyce? Thus I have retained two of the errors spotted by Len during his scan of my memoir. Taking a page out of James Joyce's literary techniques seemed like good advice offered by Len.

Mulling over Len's comments, I would welcome the term versatile be added to peripatetic, eclectic, eccentric, curious and as crazy as an outhouse rat. With all modesty, I'd also like to think of myself as an accomplished writer and observer of life. I know that Len would agree with these qualities as well. I have bolstered my 'thin' travel writing by adding several experiences which had previously slipped beneath my peripatetic radar.

The first dates back to approximately the year 2000: Pierre Oger was a French-Canadian teaching colleague who was in charge of the cooking program at Orangeville District Secondary School. Piere and I often hiked together on the Bruce Trail near Orangeville while we both taught. Following his retirement, Pierre invited me to participate in a trout fishing excursion with a dozen of his French-speaking buddies, many of whom were his relatives. Most of the fishermen were bilingual, but several spoke only French.

Although my trout fishing skills were minimal, there was no shortage of good advice from experienced members of the group (much of it of it good-natured kidding). Language was never a problem on the fishing excursion, partly due to my own knowledge, limited though it was, of the French language. I made it clear to all concerned from the start that my main interest was in taking photographs during the trip. I believe at times that the others who fished thought that just because I wasn't catching many trout, I wasn't enjoying myself. I probably caught the fewest number of fish of anyone in the group, but the ones I did reel in were at least respectable. In hindsight, I should have used this occasion to make better use of my fly fishing rod! All of the caught trout were shared equally by the group at the end of the trip and I supplied several sets of photos to those who wished them as we parted company. I also provided a few cartoons during the fishing excursion to add my own English brand of humour to the occasion. Since Chef Pierre cooked a daily feed of fresh trout along with a substantial breakfast each day. I ended the two-week outing with a story that I titled, "Have Chef Will Travel." My wealth of photographs, the story, and having Gray Jay birds feed from my hand, as well as the supply of trout I took home, made the French Excursion into Northern Quebec an experience to add to my stock of cherished memories. The largest trout that I caught was not worth mounting but it did provide my wife and me with a tasty fish dinner after I returned home.

This fishing trip proved to be a warm up for a one week camping and canoe trip for Pierre and me through Killarney Provincial Park in Ontario during September 2-6, 2002. I provided the canoe and a two-man tent for the trip and we shared the food and expenses. To solve our water consumption needs, Pierre brought along a water purifier that we could use to obtain drinkable water from the lakes. I usually paddled from the bow of the canoe while Pierre controlled the stern since he was more adept at keeping us on track and as well he weighed somewhat more than I did. Once again, having a French chef as a participant in the wilds to prepare meals definitely made the experience more enjoyable.

27 The Best Laid Plans

Not all of my travel ideas transpired as planned. The prime example of one that didn't was related to the El Camino, a pilgrimage to Santiago de Compostella. It was not until I had reached sixty years of age that I became aware of this walk from France across the Pyrenees Mountains and through the Spanish countryside. My first exposure to the existence of the pilgrimage was the result of a radio program on the CBC. Due to complications in my own life, I was forced to delay final preparations and my departure until I was 72 years of age. Age should not really have been a factor for not completing the pilgrimage, because I know of at least one person who completed the walk at the age of 80. Once I decided to carry out the walk, I lugged rocks in a backpack over Dufferin County roads and Bruce Trail terrain in an effort to get myself in shape. Although I am not a particularly religious person, I considered the El Camino would be a spiritual walk, one during which I could spend six weeks of personal soul-searching.

Once I had been bitten by the pilgrimage bug, I talked to two different pilgrims who had completed the trek, read at least a half dozen books on El Camino and obtained maps, travel information, equipment and purchased a return plane ticket to Paris, France, allowing myself six weeks to complete the 500 mile walk. Pierre Oger originally expressed an interest in accompanying me but he changed his mind thinking that the trip would be too taxing for him. I had hoped to follow in the footsteps of such luminaries as St. Francis of Asissi, Charlemagne, Dante and Chaucer. I departed from Orangeville on Saturday, July 31, 2010 aboard an Air Transat flight to Paris. As I prepared to leave Orangeville, providing myself the six-week window, there were reports of major forest fires in Spain. Once I arrived in France at Charles de Gaulle airport, my only fixed obligation was to be back at the Paris airport for the return flight home on Monday September 12. Since I had no one else to answer to, I decided to abandon the Santiago pilgrimage, and instead spend six weeks meandering through France from city to city on high speed trains and on foot when I could. I headed by train first for Bordeaux, then on to Marseille. After I had absorbed as much of the local culture as I could, to round out the experience, I took couple of short day trips by boats in the Mediterranean.

When I returned to Paris, during a phone call with Dorothy, she reminded me of the fact that a memorial to her father Warrant Officer Walter Hibbert was located in a cemetery at Dunkirk. It would probably be at this point that Len Johnson would say that my versatile nature kicked into play. I decided to transfer my interest from a personal pilgrimage through Spain to a spiritual one for Dorothy to scout out the cemetery in Dunkirk where her father was honoured.

From Paris's Charles de Gaulle Airport I made the trip by train to Calais the closest large city to Dunkirk. I spent a week there during which I travelled by bus 30 miles to Dunkirk and managed to locate the column upon which Dorothy's father's name was inscribed. I returned from France with a collection of unique travel photos and photos from the Dunkirk cemetery providing some closure to the life of Warrant Officer Hibbert who was one of the casualties of the Second World War and the Dunkirk withdrawal. This allowed me to complete the following story which was printed in the Orangeville Banner newspaper on Remembrance Day 2010.

Missing in Action

Why was I relaxing on a beach this summer immersed in the serenity of Calais, France?

It was the early morning of September 2nd. Azure skies were reflected in the rhythmic North Sea waves, caressing the shore. Clouds and mist on the other side of the English Channel drifted across the distant Cliffs of Dover causing the ivory-studded coast to fade in and out of view as if by magic. This was surely an opportunity to muse undisturbed, if I could ignore the squawks of disrespectful gulls drifting in the air currents, then settling to leave their webbed signatures in the seemingly endless expanse of sand.

The skirl of bagpipes suddenly rent my seamless veil of thought. But, strangely the vibrating notes did not disturb my meditative mood. The pipes which once led men into battle seemed to provide a focus for my thoughts. Angus McFarland, a displaced Scott then living in Normandy, had begun his traditional morning pace along the seawall, sharpening his piping skills. Angus later remarked, "I love the timbre of the pipes caressing the early morning North Sea breezes." The skirl of Angus McFarland's bagpipes reminded me that I was there on the shores of France to honour the memory of a man whom I had never met. Gazing across at the gleaming white Cliffs of Dover, I recalled that these cliffs were once Walter Hibbert's home. As a lad of thirteen, Walter had joined His Majesty's Service wherein he became a career soldier who worked his way up through the ranks to become a Warrant Officer Third Class. My wife Dorothy's father, was ultimately appointed to the rank of Regimental Sergeant Major of his Twenty-third South Lancashire Prince Of Wales Volunteers Regiment.

In June of 1940, it may have begun for him as a morning

such as mine, when the British Expeditionary Force and French and Belgian units in Northern France found themselves almost completely surrounded by Hitler's armies. In an effort to salvage what it could, Winston Churchill's government ordered British units to make their way to Dunkirk, where naval vessels and hundreds of fishing boats and pleasure craft, many manned by civilian volunteers, braved intense German artillery and air attacks. Back in London, it was estimated that fewer than 50,000 troops could be rescued. In spite of the German ground attack and the Luftwaffe's relentless bombing and machine gun fire, a motley group of floating vessels managed to ferry 338,226 troops to the safety of England. This unplanned and chaotic evacuation, dubbed Operation Dynamo, failed to save any of the units' heavy equipment, but was nevertheless seen as a key demonstration of Britain's resourcefulness, and determination. In the words of Winston Churchill as delivered to the House of Commons on June 4, 1940 this was, "A miracle of deliverance, achieved by valour, by perseverance, by perfect discipline, by faultless service, by resource, by skill, by unconquerable fidelity is manifest to us all." The British forces did not retreat in defeat but instead would regroup to fight another day.

Warrant Officer Hibbert's regiment was assigned to take up a key defensive position in the rear of the rear guard during the evacuation of Dunkirk, thus providing a final line of protection for the evacuees. This meant that members of the Twenty-third South Lancashire Regiment were the first to engage Hitler's forces which were attempting to destroy the British evacuation efforts. According to an eyewitness account by a member of his regiment, it was during this action that the warrant officer's life was snuffed out in a hail of artillery fire.

During this past summer, I was able to visit the British Memorial Cemetery in Dunkirk where I located the name,

WARRANT OFFR. III,   HIBBERT W. inscribed on column
number fifty-three. In addition to his name, were those of others in
his regiment who were also listed as missing-in-action. The
names engraved on column fifty-three in Dunkirk's Memorial
Cemetery, are a vivid reminder to the world of the horrible costs
of war.

In memory of her father, my wife Dorothy and I have on
display here on our wall in Orangeville, her late father's medals:
from the First World War: 1914-1915 Star, 1914-1918 War Medal,
1914-1919 Victory Medal, the French Croix de Guerre. And from
the Second World War: 1939-1945 Star, and 1939-1945 War
Medal.

The name: WARRANT OFFR. III, HIBBERT W. is listed
as missing in action, on column fifty-three in Dunkirk's military
cemetery, but his memory will never be missing from the hearts of
those who really care.

Walter Hibbert

I was disappointed at not having completed the El Camino
pilgrimage, but by going to Dunkirk instead, I was able to
complete a journey that was important to Dorothy as well as me.

28 The Times They Are A-Changin'

As I age, it becomes more obvious that as Bob Dylan sang, "The Times They Are A-Changin.'" The world and our lives are in a constant state of flux, and as fifth century Greek philosopher Heraclitus noted, "Everything flows and nothing stays—you can never step into the same river twice." I enjoy writing and will continue to do so as long as I'm able. I outlived the arrival of a good many editors of the Orangeville Banner newspaper and my editorial cartoons are appearing on a more irregular basis these days, partly due to changing editor's tastes, and partly due to more syndicated cartoons being available for the paper to use. The most recent editor has decided that my editorial cartoons are dated, and some he doesn't understand, thus as of 2014 he will no longer be using my editorial cartoons, replacing them with syndicated ones. The paper recognized my run of 47 years, not a bad accomplishment in my eyes. They will remain as part of my legacy for anyone who researches the Banner in the future. The newspaper will continue to publish my written columns even though my cartoons have been terminated.

During the past two years I have written several environmentally slanted columns for the Orangeville Banner. The following story is the second in a series criticizing plans to open a gravel pit just outside the limits of Orangeville. Not only would the proposed quarry potentially affect water supplies in our area, it will also radically increase traffic on adjacent highways and contribute to air pollution, additional noise and toxic runoff as gravel is being extracted. These harms are without even considering the devaluing of property nearby, destruction of a scenic landscape, threat to endangered species and the loss of potentially productive farmland. I include the following column to provide readers with some insight into my feeling as to how our environment is being abused by investors seeking to increase their profit margins.

Just Another Endangered Species?

Have you seen an Ambystoma Jeffersonianum lately? When the snow clears, on the site of the Melville Quarry near the outskirts of Orangeville you may spot this Jefferson salamander. You might then ask, "What's the big deal about a lousy little salamander?" I have written in the past about how the proposed Melville Quarry may affect Orangeville's drinking water supplies, and create air pollution and increased traffic on the roads surrounding the quarry once it is operational.

Here are a few reasons why you should care about the Jefferson salamander. This little creature has been an integral part of our ecosystem for millions of years. It is an "indicator species" which means that its health can serve as an early warning of pollution in an area. Apparently there is little concern that this salamander is an endangered species recognized by the Ontario Recovery Strategy. The Ontario Ministry of Natural Resources defines Recovery Strategy for a species at risk is the process whereby, "The threats to an endangered species are removed to improve the likelihood of a species' persistence in the wild." If this salamander's existence is threatened by the Melville Quarry, what is the Ministry doing to fulfill its mandate in the case of the Jefferson salamander which has been photographed on the Melville Quarry site?

The following Orangeville history might prove to be revealing: elk, black bear, timber wolf, lynx and wolverine once inhabited the Orangeville area. Older residents may remember vast numbers of passenger pigeons that once blackened the skies. This now extinct bird originally nested nearby, but the last flight of ten appeared in 1899. The Credit River below the falls at Cataract once teemed with salmon and above the falls with trout. The salmon runs were so large it was recorded at times they actually filled the Credit River to overflowing, but with the coming of settlers, their mills along the river destroyed the salmon—the last runs being in the early 1840's.

If Jefferson salamanders become extinct on the Melville Quarry site, it would be one more species in the litany of local casualties resulting from humans disrupting our ecosystem. Owners and investors think only of profits from the development of the Melville Quarry, regardless of their impact on our environment. To quote Stanford ecologist Paul Ehrlich, "In pushing other species to extinction, humanity is busy sawing off the limb on which it perches." Consider that quotation as it relates to the proposed Melville Quarry development. Hopefully if Jefferson salamanders become extinct, the wellbeing of Orangeville residents and others around the site will not suffer the same fate!

29 Gone But Not Forgotten

Since I am no longer submitting editorial cartoons to the banner, I frequently looked over my collection of originals packed in folders and binders. I believe these cartoons are historical in the sense that they represent events of life in Orangeville's history from 1967 to 2014. With that thought in mind, I presented my collection with associated resources to The Dufferin County Museum and Archives, thus they will be preserved for posterity and research if anyone is so inclined to examine them further. This gives me additional personal storage space for books. and the cartoons will be preserved after I am long gone.

My only misgiving is that I never published a collection of my cartoons with suitable commentary. This is still a possibility, but would not be as easy as it would have been with the cartoons in my possession, so will cross that possibility off my 'bucket list.'

The Printed Word

As life continues to ebb and flow like ocean waves on a beach, I'm slowing down, or as mother might say, "my get-up-and-go has got up and went." Since retiring from teaching in 1995, I have taken an accelerated interest in creative writing. My first major related accomplishment was the publication of the previously mentioned, *Hurleyville Taxi* memoir, another item off my To-Do list. In addition to preserving Howard's story for the future, the writing process has also provided me with other welcome side effects.

While I researched material for the Taxi book, I met many interesting folks around our country. As well, writing has provided me with the opportunity to stock my life with interesting experiences. I include the following article from *Sideroads* magazine as an example. My interest in birds of prey provided me with the opportunity to visit with a man whose life work was training hawks and eagles to control nuisance birds at the Toronto international Airport. I had the opportunity to have my photo taken with one of his birds and my library has expanded through the introduction of books on training and raising raptors. As well I now possess several hundred digital photos documenting the experience. Writing has thus been enriching my life in many ways.

The Ancient Art of Falconry

I could feel Flash's talons dig into my forearm as the falcon's sharply hooked beak tore chunks from the raw quail gripped in my gloved left fist. The glint in the raptor's eyes left little doubt that he was the one in charge of this arranged experience. When I asked veterinarian avian expert Richard Jones, "What's your fascination with birds of prey?" He held up one of his raptor patients. "You've watched them in flight and felt the power of their talons! Just look at their regal bearing! How could you not be impressed?"

The art of Falconry, hunting quarry in its natural habitat using trained birds of prey is an ancient practice, shrouded in mystery. Birds of prey are also referred to as raptors, a term derived from Latin 'raptor' meaning plunderer (from the verb to snatch, seize). Falconers usually fly a variety of hawks, falcons, and eagles, a practice often associated with knights in armour, mediaeval castles and the Crusades, but some historian believe that falconry originated in approximately 2000 BC when Mongols on horseback used golden eagles to hunt game as large as foxes and wolves. It has been said that a falconer needs to possess the touch of an organist, the hand of a sculptor, and the dexterity of a surgeon. Also, the patience of a Buddhist monk is necessary to overcome the bird's instinctive dislike and suspicion of man.

Orangeville's connection with this legendary art of falconry can be traced back through Victor Large, one of Orangeville's longest serving mayors, (1970 to 1982 inclusive). Vic's great-nephew Richard Jones returned in 1975 to the Welsh village of Llanrwst with his parents, Lois and Glyn. On a trip later back to Orangeville for a holiday, Richard's Aunt Dianne Large took Richard and his brother Bryn to visit the African Lion Safari park in Rockton. It was in Rockton that Richard became mesmerized with birds of prey after actually holding an owl on his gloved fist. Richard informed Carole Precious, the young woman in charge of this raptor display that he was going to become a falconer. Carole put Richard in contact with an expert as a mentor in Britain, stressing that training a raptor was not to be taken lightly, and required lifelong commitment. She recommended that the mentor could supplement the many falconry training books available.

One of Richard's primary school teachers Alun Williams was an ardent bird watcher, and as part of the ornithologists club, regularly took his students on some fabulous bird watching trips around North Wales. On one trip to Anglesey on the Irish Sea coast, the group's view of puffins, guillemots, fulmars and choughs was suddenly interrupted by a sound like ripping canvas. The students watched an adult peregrine falcon tearing vertically through the sky in hot pursuit of a pigeon, a split second visual and auditory experience etched into Richard's memory. Later in secondary school Richard began to collect bird books, and at the age of 14 was involved in training his first raptor. This male kestrel, 'Kes' actually belonged to a friend. When the hawk died unexpectedly due to illness, this may have been the pivotal event which caused Richard to wish to become a veterinarian specializing in birds of prey. After completing a residential course at the Snowdonia School of falconry. Richard felt ready to obtain a hawk of his own to train. In the 1990's, as a potential college student, he continued studying the intricacies of raising a bird of prey, and after considering what potential quarry was available for raptors, decided to purchase a male Harris' hawk from a breeder. To cover the cost of his purchase which in those days would have been the equivalent of approximately $2,500 Canadian, Richard convinced his bank manager that the funds were required for a 'new car' then headed off to the breeder! This was only the beginning of Richard's new life as a falconer in charge of his young hawk, Casper. Richard's first task was to gain Casper's confidence. Following the advice of experienced falconers, he fitted his hawk with a traditional hood. Falconers believe the hood covering the bird's eyes confuses it into thinking it is night time, when raptors are more relaxed and do not move around. From this comes the English expression, 'to hoodwink.' Richard fitted Casper with jesses (soft leather leg straps) continued with 'manning' or taming, then jumping to the fist for a food reward, followed by flying on a light line or 'creance.' The final elation was flying Casper free to retrieve a swung lure. Once he was free, Casper's training came in leaps and bounds. After two weeks of chasing a dummy rabbit on a string, (which brother Bryn would hide in the bushes up ahead and pull out as if bolted) he succeeded in catching his first one, a massive milestone. In Richard's excited words, "A bird I had trained had succeeded in hunting wild quarry in its natural state. I was now a falconer!"

In possession of his Harris' hawk, he then enrolled in a vet school with its strict 'no pet' policy. Richard decided that the best plan was not to ask permission, but rather to seek forgiveness if the presence of his hawk was discovered. He discretely built an aviary for Casper, out of sight of the residence. This plan worked well for approximately six months, and only the lads in his block knew of Casper and were quite used to his sitting on the end of the bed as they watched football on television. In spite of his care, Richard was never able to completely disguise Casper's presence on campus, as was the case, when his hawk snatched a moorhen from the middle of a well known celebrity's highly manicured lawn. On another occasion, Richard thought he had lost Casper, but a seasoned falconer advised him to return on the following morning to the area where Casper was usually flown. Richard did as suggested and enticed the hungry bird back. His other option would have been to place an advertisement in a falconry magazine adding his hawk to a list of others missing.

In his experience as a falconer, in addition to Casper, Richard has flown an American Kestrel 'Nik Nik,' a Cooper's hawk 'Lola,' Sparrow hawk 'Morph,' European sparrow hawk 'Gimp,' and Peregrine falcon 'Pete.' While training to become a vet, he spent several weeks in Orangeville working with Dr. Bill Richardson at the Broadway Animal Hospital, thus giving him more insight into working with small animal pets. Richard graduated with a veterinary degree from the University of Liverpool in 2007, then a Masters degree granted by the University of Minnesota. Although he was qualified to treat a variety of animals, his special training with birds of prey prompted Richard to set up his own practice advertised as "Avian Veterinary Services, Richard Jones, BVSc MRCVS Veterinary Surgeon." His surgery is presently located in Britain at Knutsford, Cheshire adjacent to "Gauntlet Birds of Prey, Eagle and Vulture Park" located within a few miles of the City of Manchester.

During his career Richard has contributed articles to falconry and veterinary publications, and has gained an international reputation. He recently returned from a two week invitation to Qatar where he visited an avian hospital as a consultant. This gave him the chance to view a thriving facility, and provided more insight into the world of Arab falconry which has been the centre of their culture for centuries.

When my wife, Dorothy, and I viewed a demonstration of the hawks, falcons, buzzards, ravens, eagles, and owls, at the 'Birds of Prey Park' at Knutsford in March of 2011, I realized that all of these raptors performing were potentially Richard's patients. For an update of his latest activities, visit www.AvianVeterinaryServices.co.uk.

To provide some insight into the passion that Richard has for falconry, the following is an extract from his biography. "My wife is the true love of my life but I am passionate about falconry. Falconry blends the disciplines of art, science, history, and literature with every possible emotion and allows us momentarily to embrace and become part of the natural world. Falconry transcends geographic, cultural and class boundaries and like my family and friends, will always be there. Falconry is a part of who I am today."

Orangeville's connection with falconry does not end with Victor Large's great-nephew Richard Jones. I learned that Rob Shevalier, a resident of the village of Waldemar, and Jake McCann who lives in Orangeville, were employees of Falcon

Environmental Services, a company which uses birds of prey to control nuisance birds at airports and landfill sites. Contacting Rob, the company's vice president, and explaining my wish to write a story for *Sideroads* magazine, Rob agreed to meet with me to discuss his work, while I photographed his birds of prey in action.

During a scheduled visit to Pearson with Rob Shevalier in October, I was able to ask Rob and Jake questions, and amass several dozen photos to illustrate this article. Rob who has worked for Falcon Environmental Services for approximately twelve years, grew up in Erin where he nurtured an interest in the outdoors then became interested in birds of prey as a result of a school science project. In search of an occupation, Rob first worked temporarily as a 'roady carpenter' for the Rolling Stones Rock Group. Working on the ramp for American Airlines required Rob to obtain an aeronautical license, and his familiarity with airports and knowledge of birds of prey and the outdoors were ideal qualifications for Falcon Environmental Services. As is the case for all employees of the company, Rob completed a two year apprenticeship course in falconry, and received his license. When Rob and I arrived at Falcon's Pearson office for my visit, he introduced me to his charges, among which were his falcon, Flash, birds Tally and Tyson, and bald eagle, Ivan.

In the infancy of falconry, practitioners obtained their raptors as young wild birds captured from nests, a practice no longer allowed in most countries. Rob's company raises its own birds of prey, using methods such as artificial insemination and incubation of eggs. Present day methods of raising raptors allows breeders to develop hybrids by combining compatible species such as Saker and Peregrine falcons. To train its own raptors, Falcon Services uses raw quail as the food reward of choice. During my visit, Jake McCann used his Gyr/Saker falcon Tyson to clear a flock of starlings from the 4,500 acre Pearson airfield. He removed Tyson's hood, and the bird effortlessly launched itself from Jake's gloved fist. With a few strokes of his wings, Tyson lofted into the breeze, and within minutes became a speck in the distance as he pursued the starlings. Jake then used a whistle and lure to call Tyson, back to his gloved fist after the starlings were dispersed clear of the field. The threat of the birds of prey being flown at Pearson is often enough to drive nuisance birds away from the airport, but if necessary the falcons will knock their prey out of the sky. Ivan, the bald eagle, is one of the largest raptors working out of Pearson, but even he won't tackle Canada Geese. For this task, Rob uses Tucker Gordon, his golden Labrador retriever. It was obvious from watching employees of Rob's company at work, that each treats his own special birds with the greatest of care, keeping them as healthy and fit as well-conditioned Olympic athletes.

Frequent weighing of the birds keeps them at their ideal flying weight for performing their tasks. Keeping them hungry, but not starved, ensures the birds do not become lethargic or overweight, and are more likely to respond to handlers' commands and a reward of quail. In addition to controlling nuisance birds to eliminate air strikes, the employees of Falcon Services also monitor several red-tailed hawk traps at Pearson. Wire mesh across the bottom of the trap protects live pigeons which serve as bait. An employee banded the hawk caught in a trap during my visit, and Rob took the bird back to Grand Valley where it was released. That released hawk was far enough away from Pearson so as to no longer pose a problem. Each of the Company's raptors seem to have its own unique personality. When Rob took Ivan, the bald eagle, from its perch that morning, because Ivan hadn't been up for an earlier usual flight, Rob thought Ivan was acting 'grumpy.'

In this age of modern technology, it is refreshing to see the impact that can be made by environmentally friendly raptors.

Their adaptability to the unexpected makes birds of prey more successful at their jobs than any robotically controlled mechanical ones might be. Some airports use explosive devices to frighten away nuisance birds, but explosions are no longer effective once gulls become accustomed to the sounds. Falcon Environmental Services is one of the largest such companies in North America. In addition to Pearson, they service airports in California, New York, New Jersey, Trenton, Shearwater, and Montreal's Trudeau.

Besides helping reduce bird strikes at airports, Rob's company also controls nuisance birds at land fill sites and hospital waste disposal areas, since gulls may transfer refuse from storage areas to nearby neighbourhoods. Falcon Service's birds have been pressed into service in the entertainment business as well as their jobs at airports and dumps. Employee Darren Smith has handled raptors for flying demonstrations at Toronto's Mediaeval Festival. Early in his career, Rob Shevalier had the opportunity to work with the Canadian Opera Company performing in the Czech opera, 'The House of the Living Dead.\,' an opera about prison life. Wearing a prisoner's scruffy uniform, and with his head shaved, Rob appeared on stage with his two Harris' hawks as part of the show. Rob remarked that several famous Czech opera stars were miffed because Rob and his hawks shared a bigger dressing room than the Czechs themselves did.

In 1962 when author Rachel Carson published her book, 'Silent Spring,' it alerted the world to the environmental and human dangers of the indiscriminate use of pesticides such as DDT and 2,4-D. The loss of bald eagles, falcons, hawks, and ospreys was the environmental equivalent of the 'canary in the coal mine' as their depletion signalled the worsening of the environment due to excessive use of pesticides. It is only recently that threatened species have been recovering. Bald eagles have returned to Alaska and British Columbia, and a recent edition of the

Orangeville Banner featured a photo of a migrating bald eagle which had settled down in a reader's back yard. On the top of a pole in Orangeville's Island Lake, a pair of ospreys have established a nest on a platform provided for that purpose.

Farmer Jim Conley who lives on Winston Churchill Road south of Orangeville recently took me to view a colony of almost two dozen osprey nests in a secluded wooded area near his farm. I was able to photograph the ospreys and their nest at the Island Lake location, but since it was late November when Jim and I visited the Winston Churchill site, only the empty nests remained, the birds having migrated south to sunnier climes, along the northern shore of the Gulf of Mexico. In the mornings during the summer, Jim would often see ospreys winging their way towards Orangeville's Island Lake where fish were more available. While working his fields, Jim has also been entertained by a red-tailed hawk which would sit waiting for him to move another bale of hay, thereby exposing a rodent for the hawk's next meal. Jim's barn provided a haven for pigeons, but a tiny sparrow hawk in search of another snack, found it an ideal hunting ground. The hawk entered the barn and fired inside along the rafter while the pigeons, scrambling for an exit to safety outside, bounced around like ping-pong balls.

An awareness of the part that birds of prey and the ancient art of falconry play in our lives is still alive and well in Orangeville due to enthusiasts Richard Jones, Rob Shevalier, Jake McCann and Jim Conley. Raptors such as ospreys, red-tailed and sparrow hawks, Mono Cliffs Turkey vultures, barn owls, and bald eagles, all visible in the Orangeville area, are signs that ours is still an environmentally sound one. To quote Rachel Carson, "It seems reasonable to believe that the more clearly we can focus our attention on the wonders and realities of the universe about us, the less taste we shall have for the destruction of our race." The well being of our birds provides us with a sense of wonder and humility. They also remind us that we, like all other living creatures, are a part of the same vast ecosystem of the earth and part of the whole stream of life. Perhaps, it's time to re-evaluate our dependence on our natural environment, and appreciate how lucky we are here in Dufferin.

30 The McCarthy Diaspora

As I've stated previously, it is challenging to decide what events should be included in a memoir of this nature. Obviously, not everything which has occurred in my life is worth reporting. I have had the opportunity of proofreading this work prior to final publication. Thus like Hans Brinker, sticking his fingers into the dyke of information, I'll be able to revisit any aspects of my life to which I've given myself short shrift or need to be corrected.

Once our family left Northern Ontario travelling like TV's Beverly Hillbillies to the Niagara region, we then dispersed around the globe. I was the fortunate one able to attend Queen's University in Kingston, then eventually take up my present roost in Orangeville. I paused along the route of my educational career for brief stints in London, Ontario and Brampton. During my time in Orangeville, I wisely took time to travel to Ecuador, Kenya, Iceland and other global destinations of which I previously documented. Hopefully other mysterious destinations of which I'm presently unaware wait to be pursued as long as I'm able. In hindsight, I'm glad I took the opportunity to travel as extensively as I did while I was able. Perhaps my bicycle accident was a blessing in disguise to shift my travel mode into high gear?

Gerry

Gerry was the only family member to remain in Dunnville, but in doing so he worked at

Lundy Fence Company and took the opportunity to marry Lorraine Gordon and serve as Dunnville's Fire Chief from 1971 to 1987. As well, Gerry served as a productive Legion member and now, as an active octogenarian, still enjoys golfing, bowling, walking and bending his elbow at the Legion bar.

Sister Lola, the eldest of the crew, gravitated to Brantford after a stint of elementary school teaching (which she did not enjoy). She married Glen Hill but unfortunately passed away from dementia at too early an age.

Brother Wayne joined the RCMP immediately after high school and spent his career stationed in British Columbia where he married Frances Mitchell. During their retirement years, Fran sold real estate and Wayne tried his hand as notary public. Lately they've spent much of their time in Ajijik Mexico (pronounced as ah-hee-heek).

Eldon spent the majority of his working life living north of Brampton where he married Joan Hurley. During that time he had the distinction of working on the ill-fated Avro Arrow, supersonic jet fighter after which he was employed in baggage handling for Air Canada.

Ruby settled in Southern Ontario in the village of Glencoe living with her husband Robert Plant, a guitar strumming and fiddling OPP constable. The Plant family spent much of their married life back in Northern Ontario in Elliot Lake and Blind River until she succumbed to cancer in 2002. She leaves with us the following thoughts in **After Glow**

I'd like the memory of me to be a happy one,
I'd like to leave an afterglow of smiles when day is done.
I'd like to leave an echo whispering softly down the ways,
Of happy times and laughing times and bright and sunny days,
I'd like the tears of those who grieve to dry before the sun,
Of happy memories that I leave behind when my day is done.

Brother Vance whose birthday fell on May 24, was five years my senior. Vance spent his early working life as a farmer employed by Stanley Wilkie whose farm was located north of Brampton near the village of Tullamore. If Vance had had the opportunity, I'm sure his desire in life was to own his own farm, however he ended up as a labourer in Brantford where he married Sharron Bee. Vance proved to be the third family casualty, when he died in 2009 from emphysema, possibly initiated by his habit of cigarette smoking.

Most of my siblings were quite prolific, with the exception of the two youngest boys. Vance's daughter Catherine died as an infant, while our daughter Margaret continues to offer Dorothy and me with supposedly welcome advice. My age is rapidly approaching four score years while Gerry, Eldon and Wayne are already members of that octogenarian set. Wayne's life was recently extended through the installation of a pacemaker while my wife Dorothy was fitted with a metallic upper left shoulder replacement which compensated for a badly fractured upper arm as the result of a slip and fall during the winter of 2011 at Casino Rama in Orillia. At present neither Gerry, Eldon, nor I are fitted with any bionic parts to prolong our lives.

It is always easy to complain about what we can no longer can do as we age rather than celebrate those things we still can. My priorities will obviously change as time marches on, but of one thing we can be proud of as a family is the wonderful set of parents with which we were graced. I'm not sure what the future holds but whatever it is, I refuse to sit on the sidelines of life as a spectator, but will continue to make myself heard and exercise all of my remaining talents to be involved in life as long as I'm able, even up to the age of at least a century (God willing).

31 So What?

How would I really like to be remembered in life? There are 'givers' and 'takers' in the world and I have done my best to be one of the former, rather than the latter. I was one of the first Big Brothers in the Orangeville area and have been a participant in the Friendly Visits program, spending many weeks visiting Orangeville resident Aubrey King, previously from Cornerbrook Newfoundland. Aubrey had the equivalent of a Grade Three education, but consistently defeated me in checkers. Putting my bruised pride aside, I have a great respect for seniors, possibly originating from my days working as a kid for Russell Daley of Jerseydale Farm Dairy. As a member of the Dufferin Group of storytellers, I cherish the opportunity to tell stories to seniors at the Dufferin Oaks retirement home in Shelburne. Hopefully they learn as much from me as I do from them.

In an article 'The Confessions of an Editorial Cartoonist' which I wrote for the Orangeville Banner's *Sideroads* magazine, I made the statement, "I can't imagine life without humour." Humour comes in many forms, but one of my earliest exposures to humour took place in Schumacher at the McIntyre arena. As a kid, clowns with the Ringling Brothers Barnum & Bailey Circus, was one of the highlights for me of this extravaganza. With giant noses, fuzzy hair, floppy shoes, pushing baby buggies, dogs, back-firing jalopies and antics galore, clowns were a feature that I would never forget. At various times in my life I have entertained the idea of attending a clown school, but never followed that intention through.

During my teaching career, I frequently served as a master-of-ceremonies for various faculty functions which included a 'roast' for retiring principal Jack McFadden as well as 'roasts' for other retiring colleagues. For Jack's 'roast' I supplied each presenter with a set of glasses to which was attached a large snoz and moustache. This was to allow Jack to feel more at home with his own oversized proboscis. I haven't learned yet when to tame my verbosity as was the case at one teacher's roast when I was bodily dragged off the stage due to my excessive blathering.

I sometimes put my lip in gear prior to engaging my brain, but it hasn't yet gotten me into serious trouble from which I can't extricate myself. During an event related to computers at the Dufferin County Board of Education office, Superintendent of Education, Grant Evans, was giving a long-winded introduction which he ended with the comment, "this may be the stupidest thing that I've ever done . . ." With no hesitation, I blurted out, "Do you want to take a poll?" The principals and other department heads in attendance burst into gales of laughter. I'm sure that I had just expressed what they were all privately thinking. Fortunately Grant had a sense of humour and chuckled at my comment. He did get back at me later asking for an assessment of his program, but it was all in good fun. I appreciate thought provoking comedy routines by such accomplished performers such as Bob Newhart, or the older versions of the Royal Canadian Air Farce group, two tapings of which Dorothy and I attended in Toronto.

If I'm to be remembered as artistic, eclectic, peripatetic and eccentric, curious, and versatile, 'Crazy as an Outhouse Rat' would definitely be an appropriate descriptive phrase to add to the list as well. Boring will hopefully not be high on the collection of adjectives describing my behaviour in this life.

I don't consider myself to be a font of wisdom, but hope that hidden within this memoir readers will find in the following ten traits a smattering of what I consider to be qualities to which you might aspire: 1.Don't take yourself too seriously. 2. Remember the biblical quote, "It is better to give than receive." 3. Retain respect for your elders. 4. There really is much good to be found in the 'Good Old Days.' 5. Cultivate a sense of curiosity and don't be afraid to ask questions! 6. Practise Pete Seeger's advice, "If you disagree with something, say so!" 7. Foster relationships with others. 8. Remember that as you age, you can still be a productive member of society. 9. Age is only a number, so enjoy what you can still do rather than dwell on what you can't. 10. Most importantly retain a sense of humour and share it with others.

I have not embraced gladly the encroaching world of technology with its computers, smart phones and the accompanying social media. I'm certainly aware that these modern innovations have been having profound effects on all of our lives, but in spite of the positives, I still feel that too many admirable qualities of the past are being ignored, at our peril. It is my feeling that our survival in the world has more to gain from a healthy vibrant environment than it does from possessiveness and a search for profit. A healthy economy is important, but only if it doesn't damage our living space.

Philosopher Alan Watts once said, "Trying to define yourself is like trying to bite your own teeth." If I was to be labeled, "Environmentalist, Humorist, or Voice of Social Conscience", these would be great ones, any of which I'd proudly accept. Rather than any such label however, I believe that my true nature lies within the undercurrent of what I've written in this memoir. To quote author Ted Sturgeon, "It doesn't matter what you write, what you believe will show through!"

As I neared the completion of this memoir in May of 2014, I was saddened to learn of the death of Canadian author Farley Mowat at the age of ninety-two. My library contains copies of the majority of the thirty books which Farley has written. I have always enjoyed his writing which is a great mix of humour, nature and material slanted towards environmental subjects. When the true facts in his writing were criticized, he responded, "I never let facts get in the way of a good story!" I admired Farley Mowat as a feisty character and a great storyteller, one with a unique personality.

During one of my many visits to Orilia, as I sat in a Tim Hortons Restaurant scratching ideas with a fountain pen on a pad of paper, another customer approached and asked, "Are you Farley Mowat, the author?" It was at that moment that I realized that as well as sharing an interest in writing with Farley Mowat, I also shared an amazing likeness. As with Pete Seeger, I'll never be another Farley Mowat, but who knows perhaps I enjoy some latent quality that Seeger and Mowat both wished they possessed?

Although I expect to be around for at least another quarter century, Dorothy and I have made and paid for most arrangements for our eventual demise. We own a scenic plot under the branches of a giant maple in Orangeville's Greenwood Cemetery, and since we plan to be cremated, I have purchased two bronze urns, in the shape of books to contain our cremated ashes. What better way to end life, than as two bookends? I would expect that once filled, our urns would be buried in our Greenwood plot, not left to decorate someone's mantel! I'd like inscribed on the cover of my book of ashes along with my name and birth date, the title, *"Mac's On The Road Again-still curious."* On the back I'd like inscribed along with the date of my demise, the words from the Rubyaiyat of Omar Khayam. *"The Moving Finger writes; and having writ, Moves On:"*

Prompted by the actions of a late friend, Murray Young, I am considering offering any useful parts of my anatomy for organ donations. With studies on concussions these days, and since doctors at Sunnybrook have previously tinkered with the inside of my cranium, I will offer my brain to Sunnybrook Hospital for research. If they won't accept my brain as one to study, it will be ashes to ashes and dust to dust with the rest of me. Unfortunately I may never know the final condition of my brain but I'm sure that as I gasp my last breath my brain will no longer be a tabula rasa!

As I mull over the contents of this memoir, I'm glad I accepted the challenge to write it and consider what I've accomplished and how my life has evolved. This is another item off my To-Do list. I remain intrigued at how lucky I've been to have events in my life fall into place so nicely.

I first met Leonard J. Johnson at the Mezza Luna Cafe in Orillia, Ontario on November 3/2003. I asked Len to sign for me a copy of his book, *Forty Years in a Life.* Along with his signature Len included the following advice, "Remain delightful just as you are. Explore every avenue as every road leads to home." It seems that even at that first meeting, Len was able to see through the smoke screen of my personality to recognize the fact that my sense of curiosity would be the prime motivator in my life which was destined to be peripatetic. He left it up to me to determine how I would interpret his phrase, "Explore every avenue as every road leads to home." I believe that these words reflect the same road as the one defined by the epitaph, on the crumbling tombstone of a crusty old gunslinger buried in Boothill Cemetery, in Tombstone, Arizona which suggests, my aim in life. "Be yourself and don't be afraid to speak up!" or as the epitaph reads: *"Be what you is, Cuz if you be what you ain't, then you ain't what you is."*

Mac, A Minnie Biography

William Clare McCarthy (aka Mac) was born April 19, 1939 in the Northern Ontario Hamlet of Gold Centre, several miles south of Timmins. In approximately 1945, the family of nine (5 boys and 2 girls) moved to nearby Schumacher, then three years later headed south to Dunnville on the shore of the Grand River, near its mouth on Lake Erie. Clare completed most of his public elementary and secondary schooling in Dunnville, graduating in 1957 from Dunnville High School.

After spending four years at Queen's University in Kingston, Clare graduated in 1961 with a Specialist degree in mathematics. He spent two summers to qualify as a school teacher, then taught secondary school mathematics for one year in London. Ontario. The next three years were spent in Brampton. He married Dorothy Hibbert in Brampton in 1962 then they moved to Orangeville where Clare spent his final thirty years of teaching. During his 34 years of secondary school teaching, Clare principally taught mathematics with a few classes in art in Orangeville while serving as Mathematics Department Head then Program Supervisor of the Math and Science Departments.

In 1967, he began submitting weekly editorial cartoons to the *Orangeville Banner* and continued doing so until 2014. Thus well over 900 of his editorial cartoons were published during this time with the Banner.

His life-changing bicycle accident took place in 1979. This prompted him to begin travelling, first to the Amazon Headwaters in Ecuador, then on a Kenya safari, to Iceland, and Patagonia. Other incidental trips included the Seychelles for a belated

honeymoon, then Ste. Pierre & Miquelon, Key West Florida, New
Orleans, England, Ireland, Wales and multi-Newfoundland visits.

During his last ten years of teaching, he served as president
of the Orangeville Camera Club and took courses in art including,
pencil, pen & ink, egg tempera, acrylics and water colour while he
belonged to the Orangeville Art Group. Clare retired from teaching
in 1995 after 34 years. During his retirement years he purchased a
camper and three-quarter ton Dodge pickup in which he and
Dorothy and their Border Collie Mirk travelled across Western
Canada to British Columbia, then up to the Alaska Highway and
back to Orangeville. The camper was traded in on a 35- foot travel
trailer which rested permanently on a Bruce Peninsula site.
Dorothy and Clare enjoyed their summer camping at the Bruce's
Little Pike Bay for 20 years before selling the trailer. He is now an
active member of the Headwaters Writers Guild and serves as its
treasurer.

Mac began submitting a column monthly, *Meandering
Through Life*, and writing extensively after retirement. He ~~created~~ *engaged*
the Moose Hide Press which published the *Hurleyville Taxi*
memoir. Clare continued to submit his monthly columns,
Meandering Through Life, to the Orangeville Banner and in 2013,
self-published, a collection of Banner columns in a book title
d*Meandering*. His latest writing includes this memoir and he is
also working on a novel with the working-title ~~Eagle Feathers &
Skunk Tails~~. *Tales From Porcupine Junction A Moose*

Clare presently belongs to the Dufferin Circle of
Storytellers which includes monthly visits to Dufferin Oaks
retirement home in Shelburne where he tells stories to residents,
encouraging them to reciprocate with tales of their own. At an age
of three score and fifteen years, Clare's latest gig is to disprove the
old adage, "You can't teach an old dog new tricks!" as he attempts
to master the 5-string banjo. Mac continues to support BookLore

bookstore by purchasing the latest publications in an attempt to stimulate his little gray cells and help stave off dementia. He has enough unread material to last him through to eternity but he still keeps buying more books. He might call himself a bibliophile, but his friends just call him nuts for doing so.

Pasture Paradise.

Acknowledgements

I wish to thank Gloria Nye for editing this masterpiece and pulling together all of the illustrations to get my effort into publishable form.

My friend, Gus Dickson, assisted with computer work and allowed a budding banjo player to make an ass of himself by including a donkey with my banjo-picker self-portrait, thus displaying the wonders of Photo Shop.

Ex-Roman Catholic Priest, Len Johnson, of Orillia did me the honour of perusing a first draft of this memoir, and supplying insightful comments which I took to heart.

Teacher Glen Godfrey created the caricature on the front cover of this memoir, and the framed portrait was presented to me as a gift by my fellow teachers at the time of my retirement in 1995.

I'm the one on the left!

Proof

Made in the USA
Charleston, SC
31 August 2015